VACCINES CHANGE THE WORLD

SCIENCE IN ACTION

VACCINES CHANGE THE WORLD

GILLIAN KING-CARGILE
ILLUSTRATED BY SANDIE SONKE

Albert Whitman & Company
Chicago, Illinois

For my children and all the kids around the world who
survive and thrive because of science. Stay curious!—GK-C

To my late husband, Marty, who was an amazing husband,
father, and nurse—SS

Library of Congress Cataloguing-in-Publication Data
is on file with the publisher.
Text copyright © 2022 by Gillian King-Cargile
Illustrations copyright © 2022 by Albert Whitman & Company
Illustrations by Sandie Sonkie
First published in the United States of America in 2022
by Albert Whitman & Company
ISBN 978-0-8075-8481-1 (hardcover)
ISBN 978-0-8075-8107-0 (paperback)
ISBN 978-0-8075-8482-8 (ebook)

Photo credits: Public Domain, 9; Public Domain, 20;
A boy struggling with a rabid dog, reproduction of a photograph,
Wellcome Collection, 42; Public Domain, 53; Shibasaburo Kitasato,
photograph, Wellcome Collection, 61; Public Domain, 66;
National Library of Scotland, 77; Public Domain, 96;
National Archives photo no. NPx 73-113:61, 98; National Archives
photo no. NLR-PHOCO-A-754(25), 102; Public Domain, 104;
Walter Reed Army Medical Center, 125.

Printed in China
10 9 8 7 6 5 4 3 2 1 WKT 26 25 24 23 22
Design by Aphelandra
For more information about Albert Whitman & Company
visit our website at www.albertwhitman.com

CONTENTS

....

Introduction 1

1. The First Vaccine: Smallpox 5

2. Louis Pasteur Saves Dairy Products and Lives 17

3. Pasteur and the First Human Vaccine 33

4. John Snow, Cholera, and the Rise of Public Health . . 45

5. The Rise of Serum Therapy 59

6. The 1918 Pandemic: The Devil Flu 71

7. The Polio Panic 93

8. The Ticking Clock of Scientific Discovery 103

9. Maurice Hilleman and the Quest to End
   Childhood Suffering 123

10. An Age of Pandemics 153

11. COVID-19 161

Conclusion 172

Glossary 177

Recommended Reading 186

INTRODUCTION

··

The first vaccine I remember getting came in a sugary oral suspension. It was a delicious, butterscotch-flavored liquid that my pediatrician poured directly into my mouth. It was liquid candy. And, apparently, it could save my life.

The next time I went to the doctor, I asked her for more.

"You don't need more," she told me. I assured her that I *did* need more because it was very butterscotch-y and fantastic. "You don't need more," she said again. "It's a vaccine. After this dose, you'll never get polio."

It's amazing to me now that these childhood moments have saved me and over eight million children a year from painful rashes, scarring, blindness, paralysis, and even death.

Experts estimate that the average American lives up to thirty years longer because of vaccines.

Thanks to vaccines and modern medicine, the first true pandemic that most of us have experienced is the COVID-19 pandemic. The first vaccine that has meant more to us than an ouchy and a cool Band-Aid® and a superhero sticker is the COVID shot. COVID-19, and the vaccine that protects us against it, have changed the world. But COVID-19 wasn't our first fight. In the twentieth century alone, millions of people, especially children, perished because of viruses.

The core science of vaccines is fairly simple. Edward Jenner, a British country doctor, thought up the idea in 1796, but it was based on folk wisdom thousands of years older than that. Vaccines introduce our bodies to something that can make us sick. When that happens, our bodies find a way to fight off the substance, and, hopefully, remember how to protect us from it in the future.

Medical researchers around the world spent the last two centuries trying to understand why vaccines worked, and most importantly, how to make those vaccines as safe and effective as possible. Sometimes they made mistakes. Sometimes they came to the wrong conclusion. Sometimes, unfortunately, people got hurt. But science isn't a destination; it's a process. Generation after generation of some of the world's smartest people looked at the research that had come before them, and then they added to it. They created new knowledge. They refined processes. They saved more lives. That process of innovation and improvement is continuing today, and new medical breakthroughs are on the horizon. New vaccines will prevent future suffering.

I grew up in the 1980s. The kids of my generation were the lucky ones who never had to suffer through smallpox or mumps or polio or measles or rubella. You are the lucky kids who will never get chicken pox or shingles or human papillomavirus. We are the world population that will overcome new viruses because of advances in medical technology, immunotherapy, genetic editing, and vaccines.

For the past thirty or forty years, it was easy to fidget your way through your vaccinations without even knowing what they prevented. COVID-19 changed that. The virus made us remember how vulnerable our bodies can be to microscopic invaders. It made us appreciate our internet connections and our connections to family and friends. It made us cheer for doctors and nurses and scientists who were working day and night to save as many people as possible.

This book tells the story of vaccines and the people who made them. There are thousands of people who contributed to every medical advancement, from the famous researchers who ran the laboratories, to the unsung assistants who worked alongside them, to the doctors and nurses who treated patients and documented diseases, to the parents and children who lined up to be the first to test a new vaccine for the greater good. The history of vaccines is also the history of public health, in which everyone plays their part.

This book also tells about diseases that are now preventable because of vaccines. Vaccines have changed our lives. Many of the diseases explored in this book are still lurking in the world. We can prevent them from creeping back into our lives with only a few shots, a few moments of annoyance, and slight discomfort.

This book is a celebration, a testament to the idea that by working hard and trusting science, we can save lives.

CHAPTER 1

THE FiRST VaCCiNE: SMallPeX

Disease Demons and Milkmaids

Long before humanity started wearing masks, before we realized that germs make us sick, before we invented the microscope to peer at the tiny single-celled organisms inhabiting our world, we understood one thing about human health: Smallpox was one of the worst things that could happen to you.

You had a high fever, you felt exhausted, your head and back ached, and your body was covered with a red rash that burned. Over the next few weeks, the rash erupted with hard, raised, rounded blisters that wept pus. This painful agony lasted about three or four weeks until the blisters dried up, scabbed over, and fell away. You could suffer scarring or maybe even blindness. Experts estimate that as many as 30 percent of people who contracted smallpox did not survive. And the number of people who caught smallpox was high. One infected person usually spread the disease to about five others.

There was no cure for smallpox.

There is still no cure for smallpox.

Historians believe that the disease ran rampant through humanity for the past twelve thousand years. Evidence of smallpox scars have been found on three-thousand-year-old mummies of Egyptian pharaohs. Smallpox plagues severely weakened Ancient Rome. One epidemic is believed to have circulated throughout the empire for fifteen years, from 165 to 180 CE, killing nearly one-third of Rome's population and halting the spread of the Roman Empire throughout Europe.

Smallpox became so widespread that several cultures worshipped smallpox as a wrathful deity or an angry spirit. In China, it was believed that the goddess T'ou-Shen Niang-Niang spread smallpox to people to spoil their beauty. She especially liked preying upon pretty children. Some legends claimed that children could fool the goddess and avoid smallpox by sleeping with their faces covered by an ugly mask.

When smallpox spread to Japan in 735 CE, the Japanese blamed a demon, the *hōsōshin*, for the disease. But they believed the smallpox demon hated dogs and the color red, especially red dolls. The demon was also thought to be very vain. It could be coaxed out of a sick person's body if family members wrote special poetry or performed ceremonial dances to glorify the demon.

In western Africa, the Yoruba believed that Shapona, god of the earth, spread smallpox to punish people. Shapona controlled the grains that fed and sustained humanity. When humans angered him, Shapona turned those very grains against them. The wrathful god forced the grains people had eaten to burrow through their bodies and erupt out of their flesh.

Similarly, in India, people described the pustules as rice-like protrusions of the skin. In Hinduism, this malady was

POETRY FOR POX VICTIMS

Poetry has also been a way of grieving for those lost to smallpox. This poem was written by the Japanese poet and Buddhist monk Taigu Ryōkan who lived from 1758-1831:

For Children Killed in a Smallpox Epidemic

When spring arrives
From every tree tip
Flowers will bloom,
But those children
Who fell with last
autumn's leaves
Will never return.

believed to be caused by the goddess Sitala, the living embodiment of smallpox who both caused and cured the suffering.

There are even patron saints in Christianity to help victims of smallpox. Saint Nicasius of Rheims is said to have survived the disease, only to be beheaded and martyred during an invasion of France. The afflicted offered prayers to Saint Nicasius to ease their suffering.

When Spanish conquistador Hernán Cortés went across the land that is now Mexico in 1519, he unintentionally brought the disease with him. This first contact with smallpox killed hundreds of thousands of people and led to the fall of the Aztec Empire by 1521, and the Incan Empire by 1572. European colonists continued to bring the plague, infecting native people who had no inherited immunity to the disease. Some experts estimate that smallpox killed 90 to 95 percent of the native populations, approximately 20 million people, after first contact. This pattern of colonization and devastation continued as explorers, colonists, and traders pushed into the Pacific regions, spreading the disease to previously isolated island populations.

It's tempting to think of smallpox as an old-timey disease that afflicted people hundreds or thousands of years ago—simple or superstitious people who exist only in history books or ancient scrolls. However, in the twentieth century alone, even after many people knew about wearing masks and

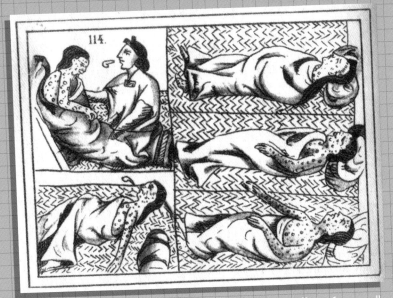

This drawing from the sixteenth century shows Aztec people suffering from smallpox. The drawing was created by a Mesoamerican artist as part of a cultural study.

covering their coughs and had a pretty good idea about the microscopic bacteria and viruses that make people sick, smallpox still killed over three hundred million people.

The history of smallpox is a history of human misery, despair, and death. For thousands of years, people were so terrified and awestruck by its ability to ravage the human body that they offered up prayers and poems and sacrifices. They worshipped a microbe as a god.

There is no *cure* for smallpox.

But there is a *vaccine*.

Edward Jenner and the Udders that Changed the World

As early as the sixteenth century, there is documented evidence of people purposely infecting themselves with a tiny amount of smallpox to avoid suffering the worst effects of the disease. The process became common in China and India in the mid-1500s and the Ottoman Empire by the 1660s. Onesimus, an enslaved African in Massachusetts, taught the practice to Puritan minister Cotton Mather, and in 1721 Onesimus's advice helped lessen the severity of a smallpox outbreak in Boston.

The practice was popularized in England by Lady Mary Wortley Montagu in the 1720s. This process is called variolation, and you probably shouldn't read about it if you're about to eat lunch.

In variolation, someone collected the pus or peeled the scabs of an infected person and inserted them into the skin of a healthy person by scratching or cutting the healthy person's arm and rubbing the pus or scabs into the wound. Another (less bloody) option was to grind the scabs into a powder that the healthy person could inhale or snort. In China, this was similar to a ritual. Girls were supposed to snort the powdered smallpox scabs with their left nostril, while boys were told to snort with their right.

As disturbing as it sounds, variolation actually worked. The process still infected people—they still became contagious to others, and many still developed rashes—but it prevented them from suffering the most serious effects of smallpox. And most importantly, it kept them alive. But the process wasn't without risk. About 2 percent of people who underwent variolation still died of smallpox.

In Europe, doctors prepared patients for variolation using the most cutting-edge methods of the day: fasting, bleeding, and purging. This meant that patients were severely low on blood and near starvation *before* they were purposely infected with smallpox. Many patients suffered small outbreaks of blisters at the site of the variolation but recovered from the weakened strain of the virus in a few days. However, they remained bedridden for several weeks because of blood loss and malnourishment. The procedure was expensive and mostly given to the rich. They were the only ones who had the money to afford the procedure, the ability to spend weeks away from work, and the servants to care for them while they recovered.

In 1756, a young English boy named Edward Jenner was one of the lucky children to be bled and purged and variolated. During Jenner's slow recovery, a milkmaid told him that she would never have to suffer through variolation because milkmaids never got smallpox. That bit of folk wisdom stuck in Jenner's mind. When he grew up, he became a doctor and returned to his rural community of Gloucestershire to practice medicine.

Smallpox still infected people by the thousands every year, but Jenner observed that many of the milkmaids did seem to be immune from the disease. He investigated and made a key connection: milkmaids who seemed to be immune to smallpox had once been infected with cowpox. Cowpox was a virus that caused pustules to form on cow udders. If a milkmaid had a scratch or break in the skin on her hands—and many of them did—fluid from the cowpox pustules entered the wound while she milked the cow and the milkmaid became infected. But in humans, cowpox caused only minor sickness: rashes on the hands. Jenner theorized that it was these minor cowpox infections that were protecting milkmaids from the deadly smallpox.

After years of observation about how and when cowpox was most transmittable to humans, Jenner decided to test his theory. He enlisted the help of Blossom, a sick cow, Sarah Nelmes, a milkmaid infected with Blossom's cowpox, and James Phipps, an eight-year-old who had never had cowpox or smallpox. On May 14, 1796, Jenner collected pus from one of Sarah's cowpox blisters and rubbed it into small cuts that he'd made on James's arm. James caught and recovered from Sarah and Blossom's cowpox. After two months, Jenner performed a variolation on James, this time using smallpox. James did not develop any symptoms of smallpox. The cowpox infection had made him immune.

Edward Jenner called his process a vaccine because "vacca" is the Latin word for cow and "vaccinia" is the scientific name for cowpox. Jenner shared his discovery widely and freely in England and abroad. It was met with some skepticism, especially from doctors who wanted to continue profiting from variolation, and from newly formed anti-vaccination leagues who worried that being infected with cowpox would cause people to grow cow parts. But Jenner's methods, when performed correctly, continued to prove that people who had never been infected with smallpox could gain long-term immunity through vaccination.

In 1802, Jenner received the first of two large grants from the British government so he could continue his lifesaving work. Jenner continued to fight for everyone to have access to the vaccine regardless of their ability to pay. He created a hut in his backyard called the Temple of Vaccinia and provided free vaccinations to anyone who visited, a public service he provided until his death in 1823. You can still visit Edward Jenner's temple in Berkeley, England. You can also pay your respects to the taxidermized hide of Blossom the cow, which is on display at St. George's Medical School in London.

By the twentieth century, Edward Jenner's smallpox vaccination was widely available across the industrialized world. With medical and scientific advances and collaboration on a global scale, the World Health Organization (WHO) and its representatives were able to institute large-scale tracking and vaccinations throughout the 1960s and 1970s. By 1980, the disease that had killed millions of people throughout history had been completely eradicated.

There is still no cure for smallpox, but humanity is safe from the disease because there is a vaccine. Edward Jenner's creation of the smallpox vaccine laid the groundwork for modern immunology and is said to have saved more lives than any other achievement in human history.

The worldwide eradication of smallpox proved that humans do not have to worship diseases. Humanity can defeat even the most ancient and frightening maladies with good science, strong coordination, and global cooperation.

CHAPTER 2

LOUIS PASTEUR SAVES DAIRY PRODUCTS AND LIVES

Bad Air

When Edward Jenner proved in 1796 that his smallpox vaccine worked, it was not understood how people got sick. The germs that make people sick were too tiny to be observed using the microscopes of the time. As a result, it took another seventy years for scientists to discover *why* Jenner's vaccine worked.

Well into the 1800s, many people still clung to superstitious beliefs about disease: The sick were being punished by God, tormented by demons, or hexed by old women with the power of the evil eye. Most scientists believed that diseases were caused by miasma, or bad air, that came from rotting organic material. This idea was that if something smelled bad, it was probably bad for you. So breathing in bad air made you sick. It's one of those ideas that is so close to being right that it's hard to shake out of conventional wisdom. Miasma kept people away from rotten meat and out of swamps and sewers, places that were perfect incubators for disease. Spoiled

food can contain nasty bacteria such as salmonella, listeria, or *E. coli*, all of which can cause vomiting, diarrhea, and even death. Sewers teemed with cholera, dysentery, and other deadly microbes that thrive in human waste.

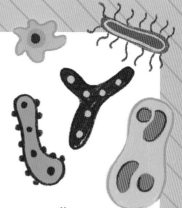

Swamps are home to the deadliest creature alive: the mosquito. Even today, this blood-sucking insect kills over one million people each year by spreading diseases such as malaria, the West Nile virus, yellow fever, dengue fever, the Zika virus, chikungunya, and lymphatic filariasis. (If you haven't heard of all of these diseases, then consider yourself fortunate.)

In Robert Louis Stevenson's 1883 novel *Treasure Island*, several pirates are struck down by fever rather than by swords or cannnonballs. When the pirate Long John Silver suggests a swampy area as the anchorage for their ship, the ship's doctor criticizes the choice and predicts disaster:

> *There was not a breath of air moving, nor a sound but that of the surf booming half a mile away along the beaches and against the rocks outside. A peculiar stagnant smell hung over the anchorage— a smell of sodden leaves and rotting tree trunks. I observed the doctor sniffing and sniffing, like someone tasting a bad egg.*
>
> *"I don't know about treasure," he said, "but I'll stake my wig there's fever here."*

The miasma theory was so close to correct that doctors' advice to avoid miasmas saved countless lives. And, besides, scientists had no real proof of a better answer until a French scientist came along spouting ideas about dangerous organisms so small that we couldn't even see them. His name was Louis Pasteur.

Germ Theory and Pasteurization

Pasteur was born in 1822 in an agricultural area of France. He grew up surrounded by farmers, laborers, brewers, and winemakers. His father was a tanner, someone who makes leather from hides. Pasteur pursued science that would have a meaningful impact for the working people of France, but not as a medical doctor. He was a chemist, and he had the help of his wife, Marie Laurent, who was his lab assistant and also an invaluable partner in his research, helping to breed silkworms for experiments and caring for patients undergoing experimental treatments.

Some of Pasteur's early breakthroughs came from studying fermentation, a chemical process in which bacteria or mold break down sugars.

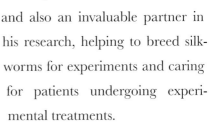

Pasteur set to work in 1856 to investigate problems in wine production. Armed with a microscope, he observed yeast, the microorganisms responsible for fermentation, and proved that grape juice could not turn into wine without them. He also studied batches of beer and wine that had spoiled and observed other microorganisms that he hypothesized had ruined the fermentation process. He called these "diseases of wine," and in 1865 he patented a process to destroy the harmful germs. Pasteur heated the wine to a temperature of about 50 to 60 degrees Celsius (about 122 to 140 degrees Fahrenheit), hot enough to kill the dangerous microbes without ruining the flavor or quality of the wine.

He called the process pasteurization, and it is now used in the production of milk, beer, cheese, and yogurt. It keeps food fresher and people healthier. According to the United States Centers for Disease Control and Prevention (CDC), pasteurization of milk kills harmful bacteria that cause "tuberculosis, scarlet fever, typhoid fever, and other diseases that were transmitted through raw milk" and has saved millions of lives.

Look at the label on your milk in the refrigerator. Find the line telling you that your milk is "pasteurized." It was Louis Pasteur who prevents you from getting food poisoning, diarrhea, and kidney failure or even dying from the milk you pour into your breakfast cereal.

Pasteur also wanted to prove that microorganisms grew from other microorganisms rather than appearing out of thin air through "spontaneous generation." Many scientists of the time believed in spontaneous generation, the theory that pests like fleas and maggots just appeared in filthy conditions rather than coming from a parent organism. This idea was still so widely accepted in the 1860s that the French Academy of Sciences offered a prize of 2,500 francs (about $15,000 in US dollars today) to the scientist who could prove or disprove it.

Pasteur devised an experiment to prove that germs in the air caused food and wine to spoil. He put a nutrient-rich

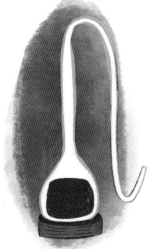

broth in a sterile swan-neck flask and then boiled the broth. Next, he let the liquid sit at room temperature. The broth didn't mold or spoil because he had killed all the germs inside the flask by heating them, and he had kept all the germs outside the flask away from the broth. They could not reach the liquid through the flask's S-shaped curve. When he tipped the flask and allowed the outside air (and germs) to reach the broth, the broth began to spoil. He won the 2,500 francs.

Pasteur made two discoveries that changed human history and immortalized his name on milk cartons forever. First, he proved that microorganisms, or "wee germs" as he called them, didn't just pop into existence through spontaneous generation. Germs were living things that were created by other living things: parent organisms. Life from life. Second, he discovered that by rapidly heating and then cooling products such as milk, beer, wine, cheese, and yogurt, he could kill the microorganisms that spoiled food and made people sick, without ruining the food itself.

Pasteur and other scientists who agreed with him were establishing the germ theory of disease, the idea that microorganisms existed and could enter the body, reproduce, and cause disease. Now Pasteur was eager to apply what he'd learned about microorganisms and food spoilage to prevent animals and even humans from contracting deadly illnesses.

Other Breakthroughs with Germ Theory

While Louis Pasteur was unlocking the secrets of the microscopic world, his scientific rival Robert Koch was using the microscope to identify the different microorganisms that caused some of the world's deadliest diseases, such as anthrax, cholera, and tuberculosis. Koch developed a set of rules, called

Koch's Postulates

- The microorganism must be found in abundance in all organisms suffering from the disease, but should not be found in healthy organisms.
- The microorganism must be isolated from a diseased organism and grown in pure culture.
- The cultured microorganism should cause disease when introduced into a healthy organism.
- The microorganism must be reisolated from the inoculated, diseased experimental host and identified as being identical to the original specific causative agent.

Koch's Postulates, that helped scientists determine whether a specific microbe caused a specific disease.

British surgeon Joseph Lister used Pasteur's ideas to safeguard people against those microbes. In 1865, Joseph Lister read of Pasteur's germ theory and knew it could be the key to curing "hospital disease": the fatal blood infections that killed nearly half of all patients recovering from surgeries. Lister was surgeon to the Glasgow Royal Infirmary in Glasgow, Scotland. Before his groundbreaking application of Pasteur's work, surgeons operated in their street clothes and shoes, which were sometimes caked with mud and horse manure from city streets. Doctors often didn't wash their hands or even change their blood-stained surgical gowns between patients. Lister believed that most infections that patients developed after surgery were caused by the germs that Pasteur had proven existed. He hypothesized that many of these infections could be prevented by killing germs that circulated through the air in hospitals and by preventing germs from coming into contact with surgical wounds.

Lister knew he couldn't heat patients the way Pasteur had heated wine and milk, so he found another way to stop microbes. He created a carbonic acid solution and used it to disinfect surgical instruments, sterilize wounds and bandages, and clean operating theaters. He had surgeons wash their hands in the carbonic acid solution and wear clean gloves to operate. His ideas about sterile surgical practices saved countless lives and earned him the title "father of modern surgery."

But even as these scientific pioneers were discovering ways to make healthcare safer, they were still nearly defenseless against the diseases themselves.

Sadly, not even Pasteur was immune to tragedy. Typhoid fever killed three of his five children, leading Pasteur to tackle one of the most important scientific questions of the day: How do you prevent people and animals from getting sick in the first place?

Chance, Luck, and Chicken Cholera

In 1877, Louis Pasteur began testing his germ theory of disease. Through veterinarian Henri Toussaint, Pasteur got a sample of the bacteria that causes chicken cholera. Chicken cholera, or fowl cholera, is a deadly infection that effects chickens, turkeys, ducks, geese, raptors, and even canaries. It can kill an infected bird in six to twelve hours. It is also highly contagious and, if left untreated, can sweep through a bird population, killing about 80 percent of a flock.

Pasteur and his colleagues spent two years isolating the bacteria and maintaining it in a series of broth cultures. The team kept some of the broth cultures in vials stoppered with cotton-wool plugs so that some air could pass through the plugs, dry the culture, and in theory, weaken the virulence of the disease. Virulence is the measure of how severe a disease is, or how sick it will make its host. Pasteur's team tested the cultures on healthy chickens, monitoring how sick they got. If the chickens survived, the scientists exposed them to the disease again to see if they were immune to future infections.

Pasteur's big breakthrough can be credited to a happy accident. He left the lab for vacation, instructing his assistant, microbiologist Charles Chamberland, to inject some chickens with one of the experimental chicken cholera cultures. Chamberland, also leaving for vacation, forgot to do it. When he returned to the lab a month later, he injected the chickens with the now-dried, month-old bacteria. The chickens had a mild reaction and then recovered completely. Chamberland thought the experiment was another flop and planned to start over with new chickens and fresh bacteria, but Pasteur had a hunch. He injected the chickens with a fresh, live form of chicken cholera. The disease should have killed them within hours. Instead, none of the chickens got sick. Because of the mild infection from the weakened bacteria, the chickens were immune to chicken cholera.

This mistake, which happened because very smart scientists were rushing to leave for vacation, changed the course of history and the way that scientists approach the creation of vaccines.

Pasteur and his colleagues had created "attenuation": growing generation after generation of germs in a lab to weaken them over time. Vaccines created with attenuated germs help the body learn to recognize and destroy a disease. The germs are still alive and still trigger a response in the immune system, but they are not strong enough to actually cause the disease.

Pasteur paid tribute to Edward Jenner by calling his chicken cholera inoculation a vaccine. His breakthrough was also significant because it was the first time that scientists successfully created a vaccine in a lab. Edward Jenner's smallpox vaccine had used material he found in nature: cowpox.

Cursed Fields and Field Trials

Having grown up in rural France, Pasteur was familiar with the diseases that afflicted agricultural communities. So he set his sights on a new target: anthrax, a disease that infects livestock like cattle, sheep, horses, and goats, but can also be found in deer, reindeer, antelope, and even camels. Anthrax can also spread to humans.

Today, mild anthrax infections of the skin can be treated with antibiotics, but in Pasteur's time anthrax killed hundreds of thousands of animals and people each year. The disease is caused by tiny, colorless, odorless, tasteless spores from the bacteria *Bacillus anthracis*. The spores can be eaten, absorbed through breaks in the skin, or inhaled through your mouth or nose. Without treatment, inhaling anthrax spores is fatal for 80 to 90 percent of those infected.

Pasteur secured a sample of anthrax from the blood of infected cattle and looked for a way to attenuate the bacteria. Exposing the bacteria to air, as he had done with chicken cholera, did not work. In fact, exposing *Bacillus anthracis* to air only helped the bacteria spread its deadly spores.

In 1880, Pasteur's scientific rival, Henri Toussaint, tried creating an anthrax vaccine by killing the bacteria with heat, but about half the animals he inoculated still died of anthrax infections. Pasteur believed that only a vaccine created with a weakened strain of the bacteria would be effective. He and his team heated the bacteria to about 42 degrees Celsius (about 108 degrees Fahrenheit), weakening the bacteria enough to prevent spore growth without killing the bacteria itself.

At the same time, Pasteur also investigated fields that farmers believed were cursed. These cursed fields were places where livestock had died mysteriously and been buried years or even decades before. Now animals were falling ill and dying again. Louis Pasteur hypothesized that worms were eating the bodies of the dead animals and then returning to the surface of the fields and excreting dirt filled with the anthrax bacteria. Healthy animals grazed in the fields where the diseased livestock were buried, ingested the spores, and died within hours or days.

On May 17, 1881, in Pouilly-le-Fort, France, Pasteur used forty-eight sheep, two goats, and ten cows to test his new anthrax vaccine. Half the animals received two injections of the attenuated bacteria and the other half (the control group) did not receive any treatments. On May 31, Pasteur invited the public to watch the results. Over two hundred spectators gathered at the farm field to watch Pasteur and his assistants inject the test animals with live, fully potent anthrax. The vaccinated sheep, goats, and cows survived the experiment. The unvaccinated cows showed anthrax symptoms. The unvaccinated sheep and goats dropped dead within hours before the spectators' eyes. Pasteur had succeeded in creating an anthrax vaccine.

On June 13, he reported his findings to the French Academy of Sciences.

Pasteur's work provided the basis for modern vaccines and his anthrax vaccine was improved upon in the twentieth century. The anthrax vaccine is now used regularly to inoculate livestock herds, especially in regions that have had anthrax outbreaks in the past. Beginning in the 1930s, researchers in Russia, the United Kingdom, and the United States developed human anthrax vaccines, recommended for people who are at high risk of coming into contact with the bacteria.

Louis Pasteur's goal was to find a vaccine for *all* infectious diseases. With his cholera and anthrax vaccines, he had proven his method twice, but only in animals. Could his vaccines work on people? He was ready to test that theory, but there was a problem. Pasteur was not a medical doctor. He could not legally experiment on humans. So he needed to work with a disease that regularly infected both animals and humans. Something fearsome. Something fatal. A disease that had struck terror in people for far too long and called to mind a terrible night from his own childhood. Louis Pasteur decided he would put an end to rabies.

CHAPTER 3

PASTEUR AND THE FIRST HUMAN VACCINE

Louis and the Wolf

Rabies is a deadly virus transmitted through the saliva of infected animals. When a rabid animal bites, the rabies virus enters the victim's body through punctures in the skin and makes its way to the nerves. Eventually, the virus moves through the nervous system, up the spinal cord, and into the brain, causing severe inflammation and death.

The progression of the virus depends on how many times the victim was bitten and how long the virus takes to travel from the site of the bite into the brain. That means an infected person can become rabid in as little as a few weeks or as long as a year. Until the late nineteenth century, this was one of the most brutal parts of the disease: the anxiety and agony of waiting, of wondering if the tickle in the back of your throat was the first signal that rabies had at last attacked your brain.

Louis Pasteur's childhood dreams didn't involve finding a cure for rabies or any other diseases. But disease stalked close and struck painfully near throughout his life. Pasteur was eight when a rabid wolf terrorized his village. The crazed animal attacked eight people before it was put down.

All the afflicted villagers eventually died of the disease.

Because back then, rabies was fatal.

Always.

Pasteur changed that.

The Sixtieth Rabbit

Louis Pasteur was not the first scientist to investigate rabies. Most notably, in 1879, health expert and veterinarian Pierre Victor Galtier made several important discoveries about the disease. He determined how it spread from animal to animal. He also discovered that it was less dangerous in rabbits than dogs. Rabbits were less likely to bite, and the incubation period was shorter, so he could study generations of the disease in less time. In 1881, Galtier became the first person to create a rabies vaccine for animals when he injected the saliva of a rabid dog into the veins of healthy sheep. The sheep became immune to rabies.

Pasteur and his assistant Émile Roux believed they could improve on Galtier's findings. They wanted to create a vaccine that would not only prevent rabies but could also cure it in people and animals who were already infected. Roux was a trained physician who had first assisted Pasteur as an animal inoculator and had contributed to Pasteur's research on chicken cholera and anthrax. Because Roux was a licensed physician, he could legally perform experimental treatments on humans.

When Pasteur and Roux discovered that rabies affected the brain and nervous system of its host, they concluded they could make their vaccine with material extracted from an infected animal's spinal column. They also hypothesized that the best way to develop a lab-created vaccine that worked consistently was through attenuation. In addition to exposing germs to heat or air, as they had done with chicken cholera and anthrax, they also experimented with passing the virus through different types of animals to see whether it became weaker or stronger.

Pasteur and his colleagues observed that a strain of rabies might be extremely virulent in a dog, but it became weaker when passed from the dog to a monkey. When they passed the disease to a second monkey, the disease became even weaker. They also noted that rabies became more virulent when passed to a rabbit and became stronger and deadlier with each new rabbit they infected.

Pasteur and Roux created a new version of the virus that was extremely virulent in rabbits but less dangerous to humans. Now they needed to weaken it enough so that it wouldn't kill a dog or human host.

VIRUSES

Louis Pasteur called rabies a virus just as Edward Jenner called cowpox a virus but neither of them actually knew what a virus was. The word *virus* is from the Latin word for "poisonous secretion." Virus has been used since the fourteenth century to describe something that made people sick. Louis Pasteur could see and study bacteria through the microscopes of his time, but he couldn't see something as small as the microbes we now know as viruses.

In the 1890s, Russian botanist Dmitri Ivanovsky and Dutch microbiologist Martinus Beijerinck both separately theorized that something smaller than bacteria had to be infecting tobacco plants, but they still couldn't see or prove their theories. Scientists wouldn't prove the existence of viruses until Wendell Meredith Stanley invented the electron microscope in 1931. This was the first tool that allowed humans to see something as tiny as a virus.

As they had done with chicken cholera, Pasteur's team used air to dry the infected animal material. In this case, they used infected spinal material from the sixtieth rabbit. Pasteur hypothesized that it was best to perform the inoculation through a series of shots. First, he injected an infected animal with material from the least virulent (and longest attenuated) sample. From there, the virulence of the shots increased over a period of twelve days. The final injection contained the most virulent sample. Pasteur believed this series of shots would help the body build resistance, or immunity, to the invading organism.

SENSATIONAL SCIENCE

By the 1880s, Louis Pasteur was famous throughout Europe. He gave public updates on his rabies research. But, just as in Edward Jenner's time, people protested Pasteur's quest for a vaccine. Antivaccination leagues argued that the best way to fight any disease was to be healthy, not introduce something foreign into your body. They criticized Pasteur because his lab did research on live animals.

But these protests spurred public support for Pasteur. He partnered with dog pounds and veterinarians across Paris to find and house rabid dogs. He even received letters from citizens volunteering to become human test subjects. Pasteur hated causing needless suffering in test animals and maintained good conditions in his labs.

Pasteur tested his technique on fifty dogs, injecting the live rabies virus directly into the dogs' brains. None of the dogs contracted rabies. The rabies vaccine was a success…in dogs.

Pasteur believed his vaccine protocol could also work for humans. In March 1885, he wrote to a childhood friend, saying,

I have not yet dared to treat humans bitten by rabid dogs. But the time to do it may not be far off, and I would really like to begin with myself, that is, to inoculate myself with rabies and then stop its effects, for I am beginning to feel very competent and sure of my findings.

Pasteur's more cautious collaborator, Émile Roux, worried that they didn't have enough data to conduct human trials. The case of a young boy named Joseph Meister settled the argument.

On July 6, 1885, Joseph Meister and his mother came to Pasteur's lab. Two days earlier, Joseph had been severely bitten on his hand, thighs, and legs by a rabid dog. Pasteur consulted with physicians Alfred Vulpian and Jacques-Joseph

Grancher. Grancher was head of the pediatric clinic at the children's hospital. The three experts examined Joseph's deep wounds and agreed that, without treatment, he would die of rabies. They started Pasteur's treatment that very night. Doctors Vulpian and Grancher administered the vaccine while Pasteur supervised.

Joseph received thirteen inoculations over the next ten days. Between treatments, he played with the healthy chickens, rabbits, and mice at Pasteur's lab. Pasteur and his colleagues kept Joseph under close observation for several weeks. By August, Pasteur was confident that the treatment was a success. Louis Pasteur had cured Joseph Meister of rabies and spared him from a horrendous death.

Rabies had caused so much fear and suffering for so long that when Louis Pasteur announced his findings to the Academy of Sciences on October 26, 1885, the doctors and scientists immediately called for Pasteur to create a treatment center to save those infected with rabies. By the end of that year, Pasteur's treatment had saved eighty-five people from the disease. News of the cure spread quickly, and infected people journeyed from as far away as Russia and the United States to receive the rabies vaccine at Pasteur's rabies treatment center. Pasteur's center offered the rabies vaccine free of charge to anyone in need and provided food and lodging while patients underwent treatment.

THE SECOND RABIES SURVIVOR
Jean-Baptiste Jupille

History books remember the first person to receive a cure, but what about the second? Fifteen-year-old Jean-Baptiste Jupille was a shepherd near Pasteur's childhood town of Arbois. When Jupille was working in the fields, a rabid dog attacked his fellow shepherds, many of whom were young boys. Jupille threw himself in front of the dog so the other shepherds could escape. He overcame the mad dog but received serious wounds during the fight. Pasteur paid for Jupille's room and treatments, oversaw his inoculations, and even nominated him for a prize for virtue and heroic conduct. Jupille was cured of rabies and also won the Montyon Prize and 1,000 francs (about $7,000 today) for his bravery. He later worked at the Pasteur Institute. A statue of his epic battle with the rabid dog still stands at the Pasteur Institute.

Pasteur's team quickly realized they needed more space to accommodate the rising number of patients. They built the Pasteur Institute in Paris, which continued providing rabies treatments but also expanded the research and teaching facilities. Since its official opening in 1888, the private, nonprofit institute has been instrumental in creating cutting-edge treatments for everything from diphtheria and snake bites to HIV and COVID-19.

Pasteur's Legacy

Pasteur's rabies vaccine and public health efforts to leash, control, and vaccinate dogs were so effective that in 1910, just twenty-five years after Pasteur's discovery, not one single person vaccinated against rabies in France died of the disease.

But in the world of vaccines, success is its own kind of problem. The more successful you are, the less people believe that they need your vaccine.

This memory lapse was a problem that public health officials and vaccine proponents continued to face. The most effective vaccines have been so successful in vanquishing deadly diseases, in pushing them so far out of view, that we think of these diseases as the stuff of fairy tales and nightmares, too terrible to be true. Smallpox couldn't have killed *that* many people. Polio couldn't have been *that* bad. But even though modern medicine keeps these microscopic murderers at bay, the threats of illness are still very real.

Today, rabies is still fatal if left untreated, but thanks to Louis Pasteur we have a cure. The rabies vaccine is now created using lab-grown cultures of the virus. The treatment still involves a series of shots escalating in potency, but patients only need to receive four shots over the course of a month to prevent the fatal disease. When administered before the onset of symptoms, the vaccine is 100 percent effective in preventing rabies.

According to the United States CDC, thirty thousand to sixty thousand people in the United States are vaccinated for rabies each year, and only one to three people die of untreated rabies infections. However, according to the WHO, rabies still kills nearly sixty thousand people in developing nations each year. The disease most often impacts rural poor populations, especially children.

Louis Pasteur passed away in 1895 before he could defeat typhus, the disease that had taken the lives of his three children, but his work on pasteurization and vaccine development ushered in the fields of microbiology, bacteriology, and immunology and laid the foundation for virology, the study of viruses. Although Pasteur never actually saw viruses under a microscope, he proved he could defeat them in his lab.

Louis Pasteur's work has protected the lives of millions of children.

CHAPTER 4

JOHN SNOW, CHOLERA, AND THE RISE OF PUBLIC HEALTH

Trouble in the Water

In 400 BCE the Greek physician Hippocrates theorized that there was a connection between where people lived and why they got sick, but it took until the nineteenth century for people to do something about it. For centuries, people took basic measures to protect themselves from disease. They isolated the sick and they stayed at home, or quarantined, during plagues. Basically, healthy people tried their best to stay away from sick people and what doctors of the time called "bad air."

In the late 1800s, Louis Pasteur and other scientists introduced the first lab-created vaccines and proposed the germ theory of disease, which convinced doctors to sanitize hospital tools, workspaces, and wounds. These ideas revolutionized the way people thought about diseases and their relationship to their environment. The scientists also helped bring about the field of science that we now call epidemiology, the study of how and why people get sick and how diseases and other health conditions spread throughout the population. While Pasteur was using his microscope to examine microorganisms affecting wine, physician John Snow was using a much simpler method to determine the origin of a deadly cholera outbreak in London: a map.

Cholera is an intestinal infection caused by the bacterium *Vibrio cholerae*. Although some people who are infected might not show any symptoms, others may have symptoms so severe that they die within hours. The disease spreads through contaminated drinking water or foods washed in contaminated water. In the 1850s, one of the most contaminated areas in the world was London, England.

At that time, many cities were dealing with the rise of factories, explosions in population growth, and the pollution that followed. London had grown into one of the largest and most populated cities on Earth, but it did not have modern sanitation or water treatment. Most of the city's human waste,

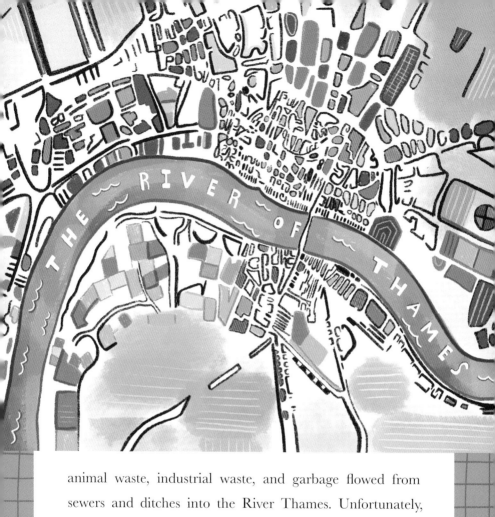

animal waste, industrial waste, and garbage flowed from sewers and ditches into the River Thames. Unfortunately, this was also the river where many people got their drinking water. As a result, waterborne illnesses ran rampant through London. In the mid-nineteenth century, the average life expectancy of a Londoner was around thirty-seven years. In poverty-stricken areas like London's East End, the life expectancy was only nineteen, and one in five children died in infancy.

From Country Apprentice to Cholera Expert

Like Pasteur, John Snow was not convinced that diseases like cholera spread through bad air. The son of a farmer, Snow grew up in York, England, and became a physician's apprentice at fourteen. He saw the toll diseases took on working people. While treating a cholera outbreak in a small mining town, he recognized the high levels of pollution in area rivers and suspected there was a connection between polluted water and illness.

When Snow was seventeen, he read of the health benefits of drinking only distilled water and eating a vegetarian diet. Having treated so many people for a variety of health problems that we now know are caused by contaminated water and spoiled food, this natural diet appealed to him as being cleaner and safer. It was also an aspect of his health that he could control. Snow started advocating for people to eat a natural

diet and to avoid anything that might make a body impure, such as animal products, alcohol, and even gambling. When he moved to London in 1836, he carried these ideas with him.

In London, Snow became a physician. He developed ways to help newborns take their first breaths. He also studied chloroform, an anesthesia patients inhaled in medical procedures. Snow created inhalers to deliver safe doses. When another deadly cholera outbreak struck London in 1848, experts still believed it was caused by miasma and treated patients with spices and chloroform. Snow was puzzled why doctors treated cholera, a disease that seemed to attack the intestines, with a chemical inhaled into the lungs. Snow hypothesised that cholera was caused by polluted water. Drinking water containing cholera bacteria led people to have diarrhea and vomiting that went back into the water where people drink, causing more infections. It wasn't the smell of the river making people sick; it was the cholera bacteria in the water that people kept drinking.

Disease Cartography and the Broad Street Pump

Another cholera outbreak in 1854 hit London's residents fast and hard. In Soho, a neighborhood in central London, cholera killed 616 people. John Snow lived in the area and began investigating where and why the outbreak originated. First, he took water samples from different water pumps in the area. He couldn't find any clear evidence of contaminants with his scientific tools, so he needed more data. He obtained the death records of cholera victims to pinpoint who had died and where and when they had died. Then he walked through the neighborhood, noting the walking distance between the different water pumps and the homes of infected people. Next, he knocked on doors, interviewed people about their health, and determined where they usually got their drinking water.

Snow found that the vast majority of people who had died of cholera had gotten their water from the Broad Street (now

C*VID CONNECTION

Contact Tracing

During the COVID pandemic, the idea of contact tracing has became a public health priority. Contact tracers are like disease detectives. When an infection occurs, contact tracers interview the patient to make a list of places the patient visited and people the patient might have come in contact with. This information helps public health officials notify people who should quarantine themselves and get tested for COVID. The goal of contact tracing is to identify people who might become sick and to help prevent the disease from spreading to even more people.

Broadwick Street) Pump. He created a map as a visual aid to help others understand his findings. He also conducted a statistical analysis of the cholera deaths throughout the city and found that people whose water came from pumps that drew water from the river south of London (like the Broad Street pump) were fourteen times more likely to die of cholera than people whose water came from the river north of the city.

When Snow took his findings to city officials, they didn't believe his theory that cholera was spread through contaminated water or that the river was to blame for the disease. But Snow persuaded them to at least take the handle off the Broad Street pump, just for a time. Within days, this simple action ended the outbreak in Soho and saved countless lives.

The same year Snow made his water-cholera connection, Italian researcher Filippo Pacini became the first person to identify the human cholera bacterium, but his extensive work on describing the bacterium and the disease was largely ignored by the scientific community, who continued to believe in miasma theory.

Snow never learned of Pacini's discovery, but he spent the rest of his life gathering evidence on the connections between contaminated water and cholera. Although he died of complications from a stroke in 1858, his theories about the spread of cholera would be bolstered by Pasteur's work on germ theory.

In 1883, team members from Louis Pasteur's lab raced to identify the cholera bacterium during an outbreak in Alexandria, Egypt. German scientist Robert Koch and his team were there, too, and they were credited with identification of the cholera bacterium in 1884.

John Snow's Legacy

John Snow is widely credited as the father of modern epidemiology. His data-driven approach to disease tracking is the basis for disease-tracking initiatives today.

Now, when epidemiologists investigate the source of an outbreak, some will use the phrase "Where's the handle?" It is a reference to John Snow and the source of the Soho cholera outbreak, the Broad Street water pump.

Besides epidemiology, John Snow's work is extremely important to the field of public health, with its central idea that everyone in a community has a responsibility to keep each other safe. We are only as healthy as the sickest among us. We are only as safe as the people around us. We are all in this together. One of the biggest factors in determining the health of a community is ensuring that they have access to clean water.

When you flush the toilet, your waste races away from

your house, away from your drinking water and your food, and into a contained septic tank or a sanitation department in your town. This system is an underappreciated wonder that has kept you clean and safe. The next time you flush, thank John Snow for using science to track the spread of

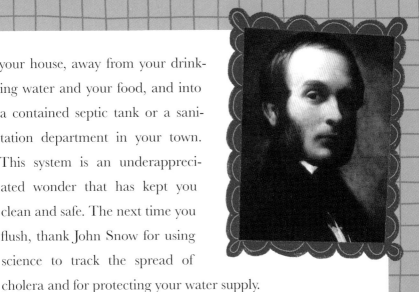

cholera and for protecting your water supply.

Vaccines are an extremely important tool in human health, but understanding diseases, tracking diseases, and stopping diseases before they spread are also essential. Although John Snow didn't live to see it, his work transformed the future of human health.

The Cholera Vaccine

The first safe and effective cholera vaccine was developed by Waldemar Haffkine in 1892. Haffkine was a Russian-born scientist who emigrated to Switzerland and then France. Haffkine joined the Pasteur Institute in Paris, first as an assistant librarian, the only open position at the time, and then worked his way up to becoming a bacteriologist. He focused on attenuating the cholera bacterium using the methods Pasteur had developed in his quest to defeat rabies. Haffkine passed the cholera bacterium through thirty-nine guinea pigs to create an extremely virulent strain that he then weakened with heat. Haffkine became the first human test subject for the vaccine when he injected it into himself.

Luckily, he lived.

Waldemar Haffkine wanted to test and use the vaccine where he could help the most people. In 1893, he petitioned the British government to allow him to work in India, which was then under British colonial rule. After a year of small, successful trials, Haffkine was allowed to test his vaccine in Calcutta, a large city experiencing a deadly cholera epidemic.

At first, Haffkine had trouble finding people to inoculate. He decided he needed to work with local Indian doctors rather than British doctors so that he could gain people's trust. He also held public demonstrations where he injected himself with the vaccine to show people that it was safe. He and the Indian doctors worked in the poorest areas of the city, inoculating people from dawn until past nightfall, when they continued to work by oil lamp. People sometimes waited in line for hours to receive the vaccine. Haffkine estimated that he vaccinated forty-two thousand people against cholera that year. He went on to develop the first vaccine for the plague in 1897.

The cholera vaccine was an amazing leap forward for science and humanity. Scientists continued to improve its safety and effectiveness throughout the twentieth century. It was not

C⚙VID CONNECTION

Community Outreach

Vaccine hesitancy is still an issue today. Some people are nervous about medical treatments they don't understand and are worried about taking advice from health professionals they don't know. During the COVID vaccine rollout, public health workers used techniques like those of Haffkine to help vaccine-hesitant people feel safe. Public health officials in the United States recruited everyone from celebrities to past-president Barack Obama to small-town doctors in order to help spread the message that vaccines were safe and effective. They also created informational pamphlets in multiple languages that health experts and volunteers used to give people the facts. Doctors, public health workers, and even family members continue to find new ways to reach out to vaccine-hesitant people to provide facts and calm fears around these essential tools for human health and public safety.

just the vaccine that effectively ended cholera epidemics in wealthy countries; it was our understanding of germ theory, our advances in sanitation and sewer systems, and our access to clean drinking water that ensured that most people in developed nations will never encounter the cholera bacterium.

However, cholera is still a very real threat in developing nations without modern sanitation and water treatment. It can also make a nasty return in countries that have had

HAFFKINE'S PLAGUE VACCINE

The bubonic plague terrorized people throughout history. It was the disease that caused the Black Death in Europe, which lasted for seven years and killed an estimated 30 to 60 percent of the population.

Amazingly, Waldemar Haffkine developed his plague vaccine in a tiny lab that consisted of just one small room and part of a hallway. He worked with one clerk and three untrained assistants. They isolated the bacterium and the toxins it produced and created a viable vaccine in just three months. Even by today's standards, using modern technology and high-tech labs, that is extremely fast.

Health officials administered twenty-six million doses of Haffkine's plague vaccine between 1897 and 1925; experts estimate that it reduced the death toll by at least 50 percent, saving millions of lives around the world. Haffkine was knighted by Queen Victoria for his work.

Outbreaks of the plague are rare now, especially in the West, but it still sickens about seven people in the United States each year. Today, doctors treat the plague with large doses of antibiotics.

their water and sanitation systems disrupted by war or natural disasters. After a devastating earthquake struck the island nation of Haiti in 2010, nearly ten thousand people died from a subsequent cholera outbreak and epidemic that lasted for nine years.

The cholera vaccine is only recommended for aid workers and people traveling to those high-risk areas where cholera outbreaks still regularly occur. Health experts say that vaccinated people should take all precautions possible to avoid ever coming into contact with the disease, by practicing good hand washing, avoiding uncooked food (especially shellfish), and drinking only bottled or treated water.

Cholera infects about three million people each year and kills nearly one million of them. It will take a global effort and all the tools in our public health toolbox, including the safe and effective cholera vaccine, to finally defeat this disease.

CHAPTER 5

THE RISE OF SERUM THERAPY

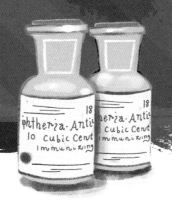

Heroes and Horses

Waldemar Haffkine, who developed the first cholera vaccine in 1892, was part of the second generation of bacteriologists. They had studied under pioneers like Pasteur, Koch, and other bacteriology experts and were making their own mark on the field.

During the 1890s, several scientists began working on a new form of disease treatment that was similar to a vaccine but also incorporated new findings related to germ theory.

This new discovery was called serum therapy. It didn't prevent infections like a vaccine does, but it was a groundbreaking method of treating patients who were already sick, and it saved millions of lives. Serum therapy was first used to treat two of history's deadliest diseases: diphtheria and tetanus.

Tetanus

Tetanus is caused by an infection with the bacterium *Clostridium tetani*. Unlike many of the diseases discussed in this book, tetanus is rarely spread through personal contact. It is found in the

environment, living in the soil in hot and wet climates or in manure from infected animals. It enters the body through an open wound or a puncture from a contaminated object. Tetanus is often associated with rusty nails, though neither the rust nor the nail cause tetanus. The rust does, however, provide a great hiding place for the tetanus bacterium, and the nail can penetrate deep into the skin, leaving the tetanus bacterium behind and infecting the victim.

If you lived in a time before vaccines and had the misfortune to step on a rusty nail that had *Clostridium tetani* hiding within its tiny crevasses, then the bacteria would take hold in your damaged tissue and start producing a neurotoxin. You might not feel the effects for a few days, or even a few months, but when they set in, death was inevitable.

Hippocrates described the devastating disease in the fifth century BCE. While ancient cultures did not know what caused the symptoms, they understood the connection between wounds and those often-fatal symptoms. It wasn't until 1884 that the cause of the disease was determined by Antonio Carle and Giorgio Rattone at the University of Turin when they injected rabbits with the pus of an infected person. In 1889, Shibasaburo Kitasato, a Japanese student studying in Germany, became the first person to isolate the tetanus bacterium.

This bacterium had eluded scientists for years because it was anaerobic—it survived without the presence of oxygen—and was one of the first of its kind to be discovered. Tetanus could not be detected in blood samples because it could not survive in blood's oxygen-rich environment. Instead, it thrived in the skin tissue it infected.

After isolating *Clostridium tetani*, Kitasato hit the same wall as many other bacteriologists and immunologists of this era.

They had identified the causes of various diseases, even successfully immunized against some, but they had not found a good way to treat patients who were already sick. To crack the code, Kitasato began collaborating with a young German physiologist, Emil von Behring.

Emil Adolph von Behring was born in Prussia (modern-day Poland) as one of thirteen children. He showed an aptitude for medicine, but his family could not afford to send him to college, so he entered medical school by way of the military. After graduating in 1878, he served several years as a military doctor and surgeon, where he earned a strong reputation for innovative disease treatment. His reputation caught the attention of Robert Koch, and von Behring was transferred to Koch's Institute of Infectious Diseases.

Soon after arriving, von Behring began collaborating with Kitasato. They began experimenting on rabbits with tetanus bacteria, mirroring the methods Pasteur used to attenuate cholera and rabies. They started by dosing the rabbits with small amounts of lab-grown bacteria cultures. The small doses eventually created enough antibodies to offer protection from full exposure to tetanus. The two men then discovered in 1890 that serum extracted from the blood of the immunized rabbits could neutralize the toxins in infected rabbits. They had demonstrated that this blood serum, or antitoxin, from an immunized animal could treat an infected animal.

The implications were staggering. They had cracked the code to treat patients who were already sick.

But while the rabbit serum was effective at treating other rabbits, it was not strong enough to treat a human. While the two worked on this problem, von Behring was working on a similar treatment for another deadly disease, one that killed over fifty thousand Germans a year: diphtheria.

Diphtheria: The Strangling Angel

Unlike tetanus, diphtheria, caused by the bacterium *Corynebacterium diphtheriae*, was highly infectious. It could be transmitted by a cough or a sneeze. Once you get infected, the bacteria begins releasing toxins into your body. You might be asymptomatic but are still contagious to others. You might develop a mild sore throat and fever and recover completely. But if you are one of the severe cases, which occurs mostly in children, you die from throat paralysis that leads to asphyxiation.

Written accounts of throat diseases similar to diphtheria date back to the ancient Greeks and Romans. Several epidemics

BOIL ORDERS

Has your town ever been under a boil order? This might happen when a water treatment facility notices bacteria or algae in a water supply. Boiling the water kills the microbe so that it can't make people sick.

Francis Home was one of the first physicians to order the boiling of water to prevent disease. While serving as a surgeon in the British army in the mid-1700s, he ordered that the soldiers "shall drink no water without it be boiled first."

of throat paralysis, most likely diphtheria, have been reported throughout history. In 1758, a Scottish military surgeon named Francis Home became the first to study it extensively. Home hypothesized that it was caused by an unknown poison circulating in the blood.

Over a century later, in 1883, Swiss-German pathologist Edwin Klebs identified the diphtheria bacterium. A year later, German bacteriologist Friedrich Loeffler, another of Koch's proteges, cultivated the bacteria in a lab and discovered that it was releasing a toxin into its victims.

At the Pasteur Institute, the elderly Pasteur was no longer experimenting with new diseases, but he oversaw the work of his proteges. In 1888 and 1889, Émile Roux began researching a vaccine for diphtheria. Like Loeffler, he concluded that the effects of diphtheria were caused by a toxin, because actual amounts of the diphtheria bacteria were so low in infected patients. He was the first to isolate this toxin.

Then in 1890, Shibasaburo Kitasato and Emil von Behring isolated the toxin, weakened it with heat, and attenuated it through guinea pigs (much as they had with tetanus and rabbits). They were able to extract antitoxin serum from the guinea pigs that could treat other guinea pigs infected with diphtheria.

As with the tetanus antitoxin, Kitasato and Behring's serums worked well with animals, but were not as effective in humans. They had to experiment with larger animals, such as sheep, goats, and horses, to produce a stronger serum. Even with the stronger serum, von Behring struggled to get consistent results in human patients. Robert Koch suggested von Behring work with Koch's physician friend Paul Ehrlich.

Ehrlich developed a method to enrich the quality of the serum and create effective standardized doses. A German chemical company began mass producing Behring and Ehrlich's diphtheria serum in 1894.

The fight against diphtheria was truly an international effort. It would not have been possible without the research of scientists from Scotland, France, Germany, Japan, and many other countries.

Doctors and scientists in the United States kept a close eye on the scientific breakthroughs coming out of Europe. New York had suffered through several cholera and diphtheria outbreaks, so the city's health department received generous support from its government leaders and was well funded. In 1892, Hermann M. Biggs of New York City's Health Department established a bacteriology lab. In 1894, he toured labs across Europe to learn the latest methods in treating disease outbreaks.

While in France, Biggs learned about Roux's technique for producing diphtheria antitoxins from horses (Roux had built his method off von Behring's and Kitasato's research). Biggs sent instructions back to the lab in New York and they were producing the antitoxin by the end of the year.

Philadelphia and Boston soon jumped on board, creating their own labs to produce the antitoxin serum. These labs were expensive to maintain because they had to keep large stables of horses to produce serum.

Before the serum therapy breakthrough, the medical profession had viewed bacteriology with skepticism, but the effectiveness of the diphtheria and tetanus serums brought bacteriology into the mainstream and brought in more funding for research.

Tetanus serum gained widespread use in people in World War I. The treatment is credited with saving the lives of hundreds of thousands of soldiers who had been infected with tetanus when they were wounded in battle.

In the early 1900s, researchers continued to study toxins.

THE SERUM RUN

In December 1924, Curtis Welch, the only doctor in Nome, Alaska, realized he had a diphtheria outbreak on his hands. He tried treating several sick children with diphtheria antitoxin serum, but the life-saving medicine was expired and ineffective. He put the town in quarantine and sent an urgent radio telegram across Alaska requesting more serum.

Anchorage had a stockpile, but no way to get it to the remote port town, which was cut off by winter ice. The best they could do was ship the antitoxin by train to the town of Nenana, 674 miles from Nome.

The only way to get the vials from Nenana to Nome was by dog sleds. With the clock ticking and Alaska experiencing record cold, officials decided the best option was to make the journey by relay. A dog musher would travel a specific distance and hand off the packed serum to another dog musher. The first musher was "Wild Bill" Shannon, who departed Nenana on January 27, 1925. After Shannon, the serum package passed through the hands

In the 1920s, they used chemicals to deactivate the toxins and eventually use them in toxoid vaccines for both diphtheria and tetanus.

The early 1900s were years of optimism and innovation. But just as medical professionals were celebrating this wave of success with vaccines and serums, a new disease emerged that nothing in their arsenal of treatments could stop.

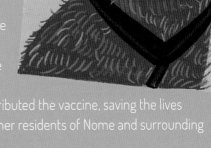

of eighteen other mushers before being handed off to Gunnar Kaasen and his team of thirteen dogs, with lead dogs Balto and Fox. Kaasen and his team arrived in Nome at 5:30 a.m. on February 1. The 674-mile run was made in a record 127.5 hours.

Welch immediately distributed the vaccine, saving the lives of countless children and other residents of Nome and surrounding settlements.

The thrilling, life-and-death story of the Serum Run captured the public's imagination, with Americans eagerly devouring daily radio and newspaper updates. The mushers and their teams became national celebrities and toured the country to great fanfare. By year's end, a bronze statue of Balto stood in Central Park in New York City. The inspiring story also raised awareness of public health that resulted in more Americans seeking inoculations.

CHAPTER 6

THE 1918 PANDEMIC: THE DEVIL FLU

The innovations of the late 1800s set the stage for rapid vaccine developments in the early 1900s. Louis Pasteur's breakthroughs with lab-created vaccines and Robert Koch's work on identifying several key disease-causing bacteria had ushered in vaccines for cholera, typhoid fever, and bubonic plague. A new generation of researchers and bacteriologists were hard at work attempting to create vaccines for tuberculosis, diphtheria, and other deadly bacterial infections. Simultaneously, reforms in public health, food safety, sterilization, and sanitation were making conditions safer in hospitals and homes throughout developed nations. But there were pathogens that we still couldn't see, study, or understand.

Viruses.

The twentieth century would be defined by humanity's fight against these sub-microscopic invaders. And we wouldn't always come out on top. The 1918 pandemic, the deadliest event in recorded history, was caused by the influenza virus. During this eighteen-month crisis, one-third of the world got sick, and fifty million to one hundred million people died as experts raced to develop a vaccine.

Viruses and Bacteria

Viruses and bacteria are ancient. They evolved billions of years before humans. Bacteria may have been some of the first lifeforms on earth. Scientists have discovered fossils of cyano-bacteria, an aquatic bacterium, that are nearly 3.5 billion years old. For comparison, the Earth is about 4.5 billion years old, dinosaurs went extinct about sixty-five million years ago, and homo sapiens (modern humans) evolved about two hundred thousand to three hundred thousand years ago. Viruses are too small to leave fossil evidence, but scientists called paleo-virologists study the remnants of viral material in the DNA of living organisms. Their research suggests that viruses could

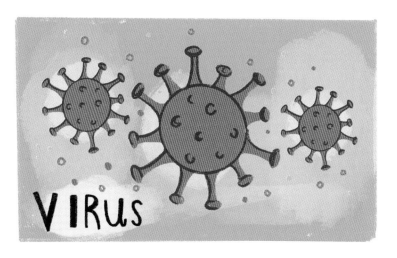

VIRUS

BACTERIA

have evolved as part of the first single-celled organisms or as parasites of single-celled organisms.

There are key differences between viruses and bacteria. Bacteria are giants of the microscopic world. They are up to two hundred times larger than most viruses and can be seen under light microscopes, which can magnify samples to about two thousand times their size. Bacteria are also living organisms that can reproduce outside of a host body, in places like water, dirt, or on our food. When they cause an infection, it is usually in a specific part of the body. For example, cholera infects the intestinal tract while *Streptococcus pyogenes* infects the throat and tonsils.

Viruses can only be seen under electron microscopes, which can magnify samples to about ten million times their size. Viruses are so small that they can even infiltrate and infect bacteria! This fact became extremely important in our fight against COVID-19. Although we sometimes talk about viruses like they're crafty supervillains bent on destroying us, viruses are not even technically alive. When they are outside of a host, they are dormant. They can only reproduce by entering a host body's cells and tricking the cell into producing more viruses. Viruses cause systemic infections, meaning they can attack all systems of a body. Some examples of viral infections are the flu, COVID-19, and the common cold.

One other important difference between bacteria and viruses is how we treat the infections they cause. Bacteria can be destroyed by antibiotics. Viruses cannot. Because viruses and bacteria sometimes produce similar symptoms, for example vomiting and diarrhea, doctors used to have difficulty coming up with a correct diagnosis and treatment plan. Now, they can take blood samples, run diagnostic tests, grow cultures, and look for pathogens under powerful microscopes.

But doctors did not yet have that technology in 1918 when a soldier at Fort Riley, Kansas, reported to the hospital building with an achy body and a severe sore throat.

Influenza and the Horrors of Trench Warfare

In World War I, Fort Riley, Kansas, was one of the camps where thousands of young men trained to be soldiers before shipping off to Europe. On the morning of March 4, 1918, a mess cook reported to the fort's doctor with a bad cold. By the end of the day, over one hundred men were admitted to the hospital. Within two weeks, over one thousand men were sick. Although no one knew it yet, this outbreak was part of the first wave of an influenza pandemic.

Influenza is a type of virus that causes headaches, fever, fatigue, body aches, stuffy nose, and vomiting. It spreads through respiratory droplets. Infected people spread the virus when they breathe, talk, cough, or sneeze. People often talk about being sick with "the flu," when they experience colds or aches or some type of stomach bug, but influenza is a more serious infection and can be caused by a family of related viruses. Today, influenza still kills about one hundred fifty thousand to four hundred thousand people every year.

In the spring of 1918, the virus was extremely contagious, but it was not much deadlier than the "normal" seasonal flu. Because many soldiers seemed to make a full recovery, they were transported to other camps for more training and then eventually shipped off across the Atlantic Ocean to join the war in Europe.

But many of these men were still contagious.

Wars have always been hotbeds of disease because they bring people from all over a country, region, or the entire world to fight through harsh, unsanitary conditions. Historically, soldiers were often underdressed for the weather conditions they faced and underfed due to shortages or blockades. They didn't have access to clean water or modern plumbing. They didn't have ways to wash their clothes, their bedding, or their bodies. They were besieged by rats, lice, bedbugs, flies, and other disease-carrying pests. All of these hardships weakened their immune systems and made them more susceptible to disease.

In every war before World War II, more soldiers died from disease than from battle injuries.

By 1918, troops had protection against some of the deadliest germs. Before shipping out, American soldiers were vaccinated for smallpox, cholera, typhoid fever, and anthrax. But soldiers in World War I faced off using trench warfare, a relatively new military technique. Soldiers dug long trenches into the earth to protect themselves from enemy fire and poison gas attacks. They sometimes spent months in them. The trenches were muddy and unsanitary, and soldiers went

During World War I soldiers spent days at a time in wet, disease-ridden trenches. These conditions left them vulnerable to infection and illness.

days without being able to get clean or dry. The trenches filled with icy, contaminated water, the filth of the living animals around them, the chemicals released during battles, and rats. Lots and lots of rats. It's no wonder that under these conditions influenza would find so many vulnerable hosts and so many opportunities to mutate into a much deadlier virus.

Viral Waves and Variants

Compared to viruses, bacteria are fairly complex and reproduce relatively slowly. One single-celled parent organism can replicate its DNA and then divide into two identical daughter organisms. Because bacteria usually create exact copies of themselves, their genetic material does not change. These traits helped scientists create vaccines that remain constant and effective from year to year. Even other viruses, like polio, stay stable from generation to generation.

This is not true for influenza. First, the virus reproduces in much greater numbers than a bacterium. One virus can enter a cell, hijack its DNA, and use that cell to create between one hundred thousand and one million copies of itself. Next, influenza is great at mutating.

Mutation is the key to the influenza virus's success and the reason it's so hard to fight. When influenza enters a host cell, the viral RNA (ribonucleic acid) can undergo reassortment, meaning it can swap genetic material with other influenza

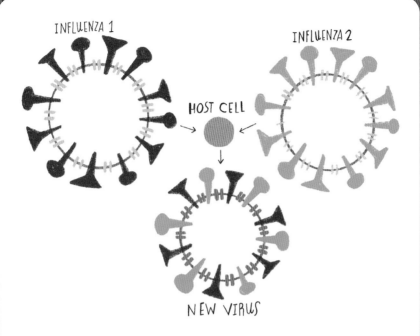

INFLUENZA 1

INFLUENZA 2

HOST CELL

NEW VIRUS

viruses that have invaded the cell at the same time. This reassortment can change how infectious the new viruses will be and even what types of animals they can infect. To understand how reassortment works and why it's dangerous, we need to take a close look at the structure of the influenza virus and then explore wild birds...and their poop.

Influenza has two important surface structures: hemagglutinin (H) and neuraminidase (N). Hemagglutinin is the protein spike that allows the virus to bind to the host's cell membrane. Neuraminidase allows the newly created viruses to escape from the host's cell. Scientists use these structures to classify different species of influenza. There are thousands of different possible combinations of H and N that would create thousands of different strains of influenza. For example, we now know that the virus that caused the 1918 pandemic was an H1N1 strain. The virus that caused the avian flu outbreak in 1997 was an H5N1 strain.

Different strains of influenza can infect several species, including birds, pigs, horses, dogs, cats, marine mammals, and ferrets, to name a few, but viruses that thrive in one species aren't usually well adapted to infect other species. One notable exception is the connection between humans, pigs, and birds. Pigs can be infected with viruses from other pigs, but they can also be infected with viruses from birds and viruses from humans. And because multiple viruses can infect a cell at the same time, it is possible for the RNA from a pig virus, a bird virus, and a human virus to swap genetic material and create a new influenza virus that no one has ever seen before and no one has antibodies to fight.

When a virus changes a little bit over time, it's called a drift. The virus structure is slightly different, but a host's immune system will still recognize it and work to fight it. When the virus changes radically and suddenly, it's called a shift.

So, back to bird poop. We don't know where the 1918 pandemic started, but we can hypothesize different scenarios as to how it started. Maybe sometime early in 1918, a sick, migrating goose flew over Kansas or France or anywhere else.

C🦠VID CONNECTION

The coronavirus is another family of RNA viruses that can be found in animals and humans. Some human coronaviruses cause diseases like the common cold. The coronavirus that causes COVID-19 was first identified  in Wuhan, China. Scientists theorize that this coronavirus might have originated in bats and mutated to infect humans. The virus also might have jumped between bats and pangolins before infecting humans. Like influenza, COVID-19 has drifts and shifts.

These mutated strains of the virus are called variants. While some variants were similar to the original strain that infected humans, others, like Delta and Omicron, represented significant shifts that made the COVID-19 virus more virulent and deadly.

Maybe that goose pooped as it glided past a pig farm. Maybe a pig ingested some of the fecal matter. Maybe that pig had already been sneezed on by a sick farmer. The influenza viruses from the bird and the farmer might have invaded the pig's lung cells and started swapping RNA. These new viruses could have then burst out of the pig's cells and jumped back into a human who was working in close contact with the sick pig.

Today, epidemiologists monitor wild bird populations to see what strains of influenza might become harmful to humans. They also track which variants are spreading through human populations. The WHO meets twice a year and uses that data to make its best guess on which strains have the potential to become pandemic strains. They create the yearly flu vaccine to protect people against those strains.

But in 1918, doctors and medical experts didn't know anything about protein spikes or RNA. They didn't have tools or tests to track viral drifts or shifts. The WHO didn't exist yet. And no one had ever even seen an influenza virus under a microscope.

Mutation and Misinformation

Think back to Louis Pasteur's experiments with rabies and rabbits. Although Pasteur didn't have the tools to understand the mechanisms by which viruses reproduce, he was creating

an artificial drift, making the disease stronger and more deadly with each rabbit he passed it through.

Now imagine all the soldiers in World War I. Unfortunately, because of the terrible conditions in the trenches, the troops were perfect incubators for disease. They were Louis Pasteur's rabbits. They were Heffkine's guinea pigs. They were the vessels the disease passed through to become more virulent.

The first wave of the influenza virus quickly spread across the battlefields and moved in the bodies of troops being transported across Europe. The frontline soldiers who had the most severe cases were trucked to hospitals and army bases, spreading the disease farther. Forces on both sides of the war were severely weakened because so many soldiers were sick, but neither side wanted to publicize the problem. Leaders worried that the truth would be bad for morale and would give the other side too much information about their army's size and fighting strength.

The first country to sound the alarm about this new, highly infectious virus was Spain. Spain had been neutral in the war but could not escape influenza. In May of 1918, thousands of citizens of Madrid came down with the virus. Even Spain's King Alfonso XIII got sick. Spanish newspapers reported the outbreak, and newspapers around the world carried the story. The pandemic did not originate in Spain, but because it was the first country to acknowledge it, the disease went down in history as the Spanish Flu.

For years, experts named new diseases after the country or region or animal where they originated. For example, the deadly Ebola virus is named after the Ebola River in the Democratic Republic of Congo in Africa. The Ebola River is one of the rivers nearest to the town where the disease originated in 1976. The 2009 swine flu pandemic was caused when an H1N1 influenza virus jumped from pigs to humans.

In 2015, the WHO issued best-practice recommendations for naming diseases to avoid discrimination against the pathogen's point of origin.

The WHO discourages naming diseases after people, places, or animals and instead recommends that scientists create generic names that:

- describe symptoms
- tell who is affected
- describe its severity

Both the Central Powers and the Allies blamed each other for spreading—or even creating—the virus. In the United States, conspiracy theories circulated about German U-boats unleashing influenza-filled poison gas in Boston Harbor or sending agents ashore to spread the virus. Military censors on both sides of the conflict downplayed the severity of the pandemic to their own sides to keep spirits up among both soldiers and civilians.

By early August, many of the troops had caught and recovered from the first wave of influenza, and military doctors believed that the worst of the sickness was over. They were wrong. Somewhere in the trenches, the virus had shifted.

The Second Wave

On August 23, 1918, the *Chicago Tribune* posted a message in its "How to Keep Well" column by Dr. W. A. Evans. The article noted reports of the Spanish Flu spreading across Europe and warned that that same influenza might hit Chicago by Christmas. Dr. Evans had this advice: "The old and infirm who are in a position to do so will do well to plan to winter in Southern California, Florida, the Mississippi coast or the southwest." He also noted that a previous epidemic of 1890–1891 had, "taught the advantage of good ventilation and the need of preventing unnecessary exposure to rough weather. It taught that persons coming down with the grip should go to bed and stay there until the fever and aching had stopped. Maybe no medication was used except a purgative and water and fruit juice ades in abundance."

Dr. Evans ended his advice column saying, "Grip (flu) for the average man, then, is not a great hazard…The threatened oncoming of an epidemic of it need not disturb our equanimity."

By September 8, 1918, a group of sailors at the Great Lakes Naval Training Station would fall ill. By mid-October, the city of Chicago would shut down.

There were key differences between the first wave and the second wave. While the first wave virus attacked cells in a host's throat (just like the seasonal flu does), the second wave virus lodged itself in a host's lungs. There, it damaged the tissue enough that many people developed viral pneumonia. The virus also caused a severe and deadly immune response called a cytokine storm. In cytokine storms, a victim's own immune system overreacts to an infection and floods the body with immune cells. Rather than fighting the infection, the immune cells attack organs and blood vessels, causing internal

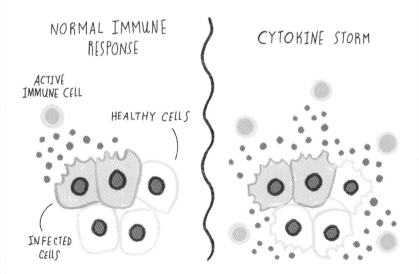

NORMAL IMMUNE RESPONSE

CYTOKINE STORM

ACTIVE IMMUNE CELL

HEALTHY CELLS

INFECTED CELLS

hemorrhaging as well as bleeding from the nose, eyes, mouth, and ears. Doctors and nurses were unable to cure the disease, but they did their best to keep people comfortable until death took them.

Unlike many diseases, where the old and very young are in the most danger, this virus hit young adults the hardest. People in their teens, twenties, and thirties had strong immune systems and were the most likely to experience cytokine storms. The second-wave variant could infect and kill an otherwise healthy young adult in a matter of hours.

Cities around the world closed schools, restaurants, dance halls, and theaters. Health experts encouraged people to wear masks to prevent infections. People who refused to wear masks or use a handkerchief to cover their sneezes could be fined or even arrested for endangering the public. Sanitation workers used blowtorches to clean the nozzles of public drinking fountains. Managers in some major cities like Philadelphia refused to cancel large-scale public events like parades, which became what we now call super-spreader events, where thousands of people were needlessly exposed to the most dangerous wave of the pandemic.

October 1918 marked the deadliest month in American history. An estimated 195,000 people died of influenza in that month alone. And people who contracted and then recovered from the second wave of the virus reported lingering, chronic

medical problems. Some people suffered long-term organ damage. Others lost their sense of smell or taste, which a few never recovered. Still others suffered neurological problems, such as hallucinations and sleep disorders.

World War I ended on November 11, 1918. The world rejoiced. Strangers kissed in the streets. Soldiers, laborers, and merchants returned home to countries around the world. They traveled by boat and train and car. They carried the "devil flu" with them around the globe and death followed close behind.

A Vaccine?

While people around the world worried that humanity might be facing extinction, doctors and scientists were working hard to identify the deadly pathogen. They faced one major hurdle: the actual cause of the pandemic was still invisible to them.

Some researchers tried to build on the work of German scientist Richard Pfeiffer who, in 1892, had isolated and described what he thought was influenza from the lungs of flu patients. He called the rod-shaped bacterium *Bacillus influenzae*. In 1918, doctors found *Bacillus*

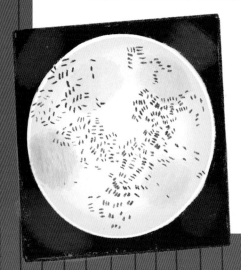

influenzae in the lungs of influenza victims and used the bacterium to develop a vaccine. Unfortunately, the vaccine didn't work because it was inoculating people against the wrong pathogen. *Bacillus influenzae* was actually common in the throat. It was only able to enter the lung tissue and do so much damage because the lungs had already been injured by influenza.

As the world's leading minds raced to find a vaccine or a cure, the world experienced a third wave and a fourth wave. The deadly influenza virus continued to mutate as it made its way around the world through 1919 and into 1920.

And then, as suddenly as it began, it was over. By 1920 the virus seemed to have disappeared entirely. Researchers and historians are still trying to figure out why. Some think that by 1920, that strain of influenza was so widespread that everyone left alive was immune to it. The virus had no more people left to kill. Others think that, in general, viruses evolve or drift toward less deadly forms. If a virus can only survive in the body of a host and the virus kills the host before it can spread, the deadliest variants would die off as well.

Unprecedented Times

One of the oddest aspects of the 1918 influenza pandemic is that it was largely forgotten or even willfully erased from the world's collective consciousness. When the COVID-19 virus exploded into a pandemic in 2020, news anchors and reporters rushed to say that we were living in "unprecedented times." The truth was that society had faced a similar scourge just one hundred years before. We had suffered through waves and variants. We had seen how anti-mask protests and virus denial fueled the spread of the disease. All this had happened before.

The 1918 influenza virus resisted all known efforts to eliminate it or even slow it down. We had faced a new microbe and we had lost on a terrifying scale.

The 1918 pandemic was a blow to scientists around the world. But it was also a resounding call to action for a new generation of researchers with better tools and a renewed sense of urgency.

We had so much more to learn.

CHAPTER 7

THE POLIO PANIC

In the mid-twentieth century, there were two threats Americans feared most: the atomic bomb and polio. Polio infected thousands of people a year, killed many children and adults, and left many survivors with paralysis and other lifelong complications.

This terrifying disease, commonly called infantile paralysis, attacked in the summer and sickened people of all ages. But children seemed to be hit the hardest. Communities closed pools, beaches, movie theaters, and schools to try to keep their children safe. The disease seemed to come out of nowhere and could infect just one child or hundreds of people in a town.

Poliomyelitis, the virus that causes polio, infected people through oral-fecal transmission. People became infected by consuming contaminated water, or food that was prepared with contaminated water. It also spread directly from person to person. An infected person could shed the virus for up to six weeks, which was why epidemiologists had such a hard time tracing the sources of outbreaks.

Part of polio's "success" was that it was highly transmittable but circulated quietly through the population. If you had the misfortune of catching polio, you might have been part of the 70 percent of people infected who were asymptomatic.

However, asymptomatic carriers still shed the virus, so you could still infect other people. You could have been part of the 25 percent of the population that experienced mild flu-like symptoms. Or the 5 percent who got a fever, a severe headache, and a stiff neck. You might have experienced some stomach pain or vomiting.

But maybe you were one of the unlucky ones. The one in two hundred who had the virus enter their bloodstream and infect their central nervous system. Once it reached your brain and spinal cord, it damaged or killed the neurons that control your muscle function. You experienced everything from weakened muscles to paralysis of the legs and arms. Maybe you recovered from the paralysis. Many patients did. Or maybe you didn't. Thousands of polio patients were paralyzed for life.

But in the most severe cases, the unluckiest of the unlucky, the infection paralyzed the muscles that supported your lungs, making it impossible for you to breathe on your own. Once you experienced this severe symptom, you were put into an iron lung: a large metal tube that seals you inside it from the neck down. The iron lung uses negative air pressure to expand and contract your lungs to pull air in and push air out of your body. A handful of polio survivors relied on iron lungs to survive. As of 2021, Paul Alexander had spent nearly seventy years living with the help of an iron lung. Able to pull air into his lungs, he could leave the iron lung for short periods of time, and earned a law degree from the University of Texas.

Polio is only found in people. It has infected humans for thousands of years. Egyptian archeologists have unearthed 3,500-year-old images of priests and nobles with withered limbs that seem to mirror the disabilities suffered by polio survivors. The first documented outbreak in America occurred in Vermont in 1894, but the disease soon became a seasonal killer, with case rates growing steadily higher until they peaked in the 1940s and 1950s. So why did a disease that had been creeping in the shadows for hundreds of years suddenly explode into a full-blown epidemic in the mid-twentieth century?

Artifacts like this clay tablet suggest that polio may have afflicted ancient Egyptian populations.

In an ironic twist to the germ theorists of yore, researchers believe that polio became deadlier in modern times because of the clean water and sanitation initiatives of the late 1800s and early 1900s. Polio was always there. People were always exposed to it. So much so that they built up an immunity to the virus without realizing it. But as water got cleaner and our everyday lives became more hygienic, fewer people caught and recovered from mild cases of polio, or had any exposure at all. Fewer babies received immunity from their mothers through breastfeeding. Drinking cleaner water and living cleaner lives ultimately meant that communities lost their natural and inherited immunity to the disease. This change allowed the virus to swoop in and infect thousands of people whose immune systems were no longer conditioned to fight back.

One such person was the prominent senator and future president Franklin Delano Roosevelt. His illness and paralysis proved pivotal in humanity's fight against polio.

Franklin Delano Roosevelt: An Able President

Franklin Delano Roosevelt was born in New York in 1882. He came from an extremely wealthy family and was a distant cousin of President Theodore Roosevelt. As a child, Roosevelt was trained at home by private tutors, away from other children and their germs, so he never experienced many of the childhood illnesses that kids usually caught at school. When Roosevelt attended boarding school as a teenager, he was plagued by medical problems, from chronic stomach pain and sore throats to tonsil infections and typhoid fever because of his underdeveloped immune system.

During the 1918 Pandemic, while serving as Assistant Secretary of the Navy, Roosevelt contracted influenza that progressed into double pneumonia. In 1921, after a stressful election defeat and an exhausting political testimony in Washington, DC, Roosevelt was diagnosed with polio and

Newspaper reporters almost never photographed Roosevelt in his wheelchair, but this candid family picture finds him relaxing with his pet Scottish terrier, Fala, and his friend's granddaughter, Ruthie Bie.

spent the next six months in bed and in tremendous pain. From then on, Roosevelt was often confined to a wheelchair, but he also learned to walk short distances with the help of hip-to-heel leg braces, an assistant, and a cane. Roosevelt fought the crippling effects of polio for the rest of his life.

Roosevelt became the governor of New York in 1928 and the president in 1933. Families and children effected by polio wrote to the president saying that he was an inspiration and that he gave them strength to fight their own battles with disabilities.

With the help of his business partner, Basil O'Conner, Roosevelt launched the National Foundation for Infantile Paralysis (NFIP). The foundation mobilized millions of ordinary mothers to raise money for vaccine research and long-term care of polio patients. And they did it one dime at a time.

The March of Dimes

In the early days of fundraising, Roosevelt's family name, political connections, and wealthy friends helped support the fight against polio. But when many wealthy families lost money in the Great Depression from 1929 to 1939, donations dried up. Basil O'Conner needed to appeal to average American families.

In 1937, a famous comedian named Eddie Castor suggested that Hollywood stars record radio commercials to encourage families and children to donate to the cause. The commercials urged people to send whatever amount they could directly to President Roosevelt at the White House. Castor called this new fundraising effort the March of Dimes.

A precursor to today's GoFundMe campaigns and other crowdsourcing fundraisers, the March of Dimes was the first large-scale charity drive that encouraged all people to give whatever small amount of money they could spare.

POLIO AND THE AMERICANS WITH DISABILITIES ACT OF 1990

Before Roosevelt's public battle with polio, many disabled people were seen as burdens on their families and society. Most schools and buildings didn't have ramps or elevators, so disabled people who used crutches or wheelchairs were sent to special schools or asylums so that "normal" people wouldn't have to watch them struggle.

President Roosevelt was popular and charismatic and happened to have a disability. This changed people's perceptions and led to greater acceptance of people with disabilities.

As polio survivors aged, they became the largest group of disabled citizens in the United States. Polio survivors were instrumental in demanding rights and accommodations for all people with disabilities and in working to pass the civil rights legislation Americans with Disabilities Act of 1990, guaranteeing opportunities to disabled people.

As polio outbreaks continued to terrorize the nation, NFIP cared for the afflicted and directed millions of dollars toward polio research so that experts could find out how the disease was transmitted; how it entered, infected, and exited the body; and how it could be prevented. Significant funding would go to two doctors working on two different techniques to create the world's first polio vaccine: Jonas Salk and Albert Sabin.

Franklin wasn't the only Roosevelt who was passionate about children's health. On a trip to Michigan in 1936, Eleanor Roosevelt visited the public health lab of Dr. Pearl Kendrick and Grace Eldering. The researchers had been working on improving a vaccine for pertussis (whooping cough). The disease caused severe coughing fits and killed more than six thousand US children a year.

Eleanor Roosevelt and the WHOOPING COUGH VACCINE

Kendrick and Eldering had been working on the project after hours, visiting the homes of sick children and getting them to cough onto petri dishes to collect the samples of the bacteria making them sick. Eleanor Roosevelt was impressed by their work and their commitment to children's health. She helped them secure government funding for their research.

In the 1940s their lab assistant, chemist Loney Clinton Gordon, isolated a highly infectious strain of the disease that the team used to create an improved vaccine that was 90 percent effective against the disease (previous versions offered virtually no protection). The team also combined their vaccine with the toxoid vaccines for tetanus and diphtheria, creating the DTaP, an essential childhood vaccine still used today.

CHAPTER 8

THE TICKING CLOCK OF SCIENTIFIC DISCOVERY

Polio Can Be Conquered

After years of raising funds and watching people continue to struggle and die because of polio, Basil O'Conner, head of the NFIP, had done enough waiting. Several of the research hurdles that had blocked the path to a vaccine had now been swept aside by NFIP-funded research. Scientists now knew how many types of polio existed. They knew that the virus was stable and therefore theoretically susceptible to a vaccine that could produce long-term immunity. They knew how to grow large quantities of pure polio virus necessary for vaccine testing and production in a lab environment. In O'Conner's mind, victory over the virus was inevitable. In 1949, NFIP created a pamphlet declaring "Polio Can Be Conquered."

But who would conquer it?

By 1950, virologist Jonas Salk was investigating potential vaccines in his lab at the University of Pittsburgh. Dr. Albert Sabin was doing the same at the Children's Hospital Research Foundation in Cincinnati. Both men were dedicated to eradicating polio, but they had very different approaches in their methods and solutions. With twenty-five thousand to fifty thousand new polio cases occurring in the United States each year, the race was on.

Jonas Salk

Jonas Salk was born in New York City in 1914. He earned a degree in chemistry and then continued on to medical school. Even though he was a talented physician, he did not want to practice medicine as a career. Salk's true passion was laboratory sciences, such as biochemistry, bacteriology, and, later, virology. He wanted to find a way to help all of mankind.

In 1942, Salk got the opportunity to do just that while working in a lab at the University of Michigan's School of Public Health with Dr. Thomas Francis. Dr. Francis was an expert in infectious diseases and the first American to isolate human influenza. He had just been appointed director of the Commission on Influenza of the Armed Forces Epidemiological Board. As the United States entered World War II, it feared another influenza pandemic like the 1918 pandemic that had decimated soldiers in World War I. The US Armed Forces tasked Dr. Francis's lab with creating an influenza vaccine that would protect the troops.

Researchers had been working on an influenza vaccine for years, but Dr. Francis's discoveries were helping people understand how unpredictable the virus could be, making a universal influenza vaccine nearly impossible. At the time, the commonly held belief among scientists was that only a live vaccine, one made with an attenuated virus like Edward Jenner and Louis Pasteur had used, would cause the human body to develop immunity. Dr. Francis disagreed. Not only did he believe a killed-virus vaccine would prompt an immune reaction, but he also believed it would be safer, removing the slight risk of infection that came with using live-virus vaccines. He knew the technique had been applied successfully in the creation of toxoid-based vaccines for cholera, diphtheria, and typhoid. At the very least, Francis reasoned, a killed-virus vaccine wouldn't have the ability to harm anyone.

Jonas Salk learned everything Thomas Francis could teach him about making vaccines. The two men obtained different strains of influenza from across the country and experimented with the best ways to kill the virus. They found success with the chemical formaldehyde. It rendered the virus completely inactive without destroying its structure.

In 1943, the US Army tested Francis's and Salk's influenza vaccine on thousands of soldiers and discovered that it was effective in preventing the disease. But it also found that the vaccine became less effective over time. This test run proved that new influenza vaccines would have to be made each year to provide immunity to the latest and most dangerous strains of the virus.

Because of his success with the influenza vaccine, in 1947 Jonas Salk was invited to start his own laboratory at the University of Pittsburgh, where he was tasked with unraveling the mysteries of polio.

Albert Sabin

Albert Sabin was born in Poland in 1906, when the country was part of the Russian Empire. His family emigrated to the United States in 1921. Sabin became a naturalized US citizen in 1930 and entered college to study dentistry, but he soon became fascinated by virology and medicine. When he graduated, he pursued a career in medical research, focusing on polio, which was running rampant through American cities at that time.

By 1939 Sabin was at the Children's Hospital Research Foundation in Cincinnati, Ohio, but his polio research was interrupted by World War II. During the war, he served as a lieutenant colonel in the US Army Medical Corps and was instrumental in creating a vaccine to protect American troops from the Japanese encephalitis virus (JEV) that lives in pigs and wild birds and is transmitted to humans through mosquitos. He also created vaccines for sand-fly fever and dengue fever.

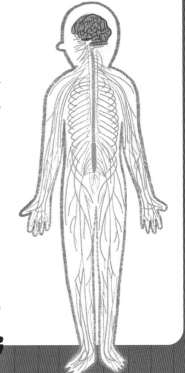

After the war, Sabin returned to his polio research and soon contributed a vital piece of information in the battle against the disease. After performing several autopsies on people who had died of polio, he proved that the virus entered through the mouth and infected the intestines before moving into the bloodstream and the central nervous system. Until that time, leading researchers believed that the virus entered through the nose and traveled through nasal passages to the brain.

What Sabin had discovered was a new virus classification, the enterovirus—a virus that lives in the gut. And because the virus lived in the gut, he hypothesized he could prevent it from taking hold there with an oral vaccine, one that could be taken by mouth. Sabin set out to find or develop a mutant strain of the polio virus that would reproduce quickly in the gut and displace or provide immunity to deadly strains of polio.

Salk vs. Sabin

Back in Pittsburgh, Salk and his collaborators had isolated the most virulent strains of polio that researchers had collected from all over the world. They used cells from monkeys as a medium to grow large quantities of the virus. Next, they filtered and purified the virus to remove any monkey cells or other potential pathogens. From there, they deactivated the virus using baths of formaldehyde, making sure every microscopic piece of polio was killed, but not destroyed. The team had safety checks along the way to ensure that the vaccine would not contain any live virus materials. Finally, they added an adjuvant, a substance added to vaccines that alerts the human immune system to the presence of the killed-virus vaccine. In this case, they used mineral oil.

Salk's colleagues described him as eager, impatient, and aggressive in his search for the vaccine. He believed he could have a successful vaccine ready within one to three years. After testing the vaccine successfully in monkeys, he was ready to move on to human trials, but to do that he would need approval and more funds from NFIP.

Albert Sabin was just as committed to his plans for an attenuated virus but didn't like the idea that NFIP was trying to speed along his process. When asked how close he was to creating a vaccine, Sabin replied that he would not be rushed. He estimated that it could take five to fifteen years for a successful vaccine. "Science runs by its own clock," he noted.

In 1951, Salk was invited to speak at the Second International Polio-myelitis Congress in Copenhagen, Denmark. He traveled there aboard a steamship with Albert Sabin and other noted polio researchers. While

Salk had the support and encouragement of the general public, the scientific community thought he was too inexperienced, too undisciplined, and not a real researcher. They downplayed his contributions to the field of immunology and claimed all his experiments simply piggybacked off other scientists' work. Most of all, they disagreed with his belief in the killed-virus vaccine. They just didn't think it would work. During the voyage, and then later at the conference, Sabin and many of the other scientists ignored him completely.

But Salk had a friend and ally in the NFIP. This friend arranged for Salk to travel home from the conference on the same ship as Basil O'Conner and his adult daughter, Bettyann Culver, who had recently survived polio. She was temporarily paralyzed on her left side and had permanently lost movement in her abdomen.

As O'Conner watched Salk interact with Bettyann, he noted that Salk treated her as a person rather than just another test subject. He saw the compassion and empathy Salk expressed toward her condition and suffering. O'Conner and Salk bonded on the voyage and found that they shared the same sense of urgency about ending this terrifying disease. When they arrived back in the United States, NFIP awarded Jonas Salk's lab a large grant to move toward human trials for his killed-virus vaccine.

1952 proved to be one of the longest and deadliest polio seasons on record. Fifty-seven thousand people contracted the disease. Of those, twenty-one thousand developed permanent paralysis and three thousand died. Salk's work seemed more urgent than ever. His goal for the human trials was to be as safe as possible, but also as fast as possible.

In July 1952, Salk and his team conducted the first human trials on disabled children, with the consent of parents and guardians. Salk personally talked with parents and school leaders and answered their questions about how the vaccine worked and why he thought it was safe. He also shared his belief that these trials were a matter of national importance. He administered most of the shots himself.

The trial was a complete success. The vaccine proved to be safe and created high levels of antibodies against all types of polio. Next, Salk injected himself, his wife, and his three young sons at his kitchen table.

The results of the human trials were promising enough for the NFIP to move forward with the largest medical field trials in American history.

Albert Sabin opposed a large-scale field trial of the vaccine. He claimed that Salk's results were promising but premature. He reiterated that the only safe path to immunity was with an attenuated, live vaccine. He also continued to complain that NFIP, a fundraising group, was rushing the science. But NFIP had already told the press about Salk's promising vaccine and had already had him explain the vaccine on the radio. To calm any lingering fears, the NFIP and Salk's team administered the vaccine to five thousand children in the Pittsburgh area and there were no negative results.

The public cried out in support of Salk's vaccine and the hope it represented. At this point, two-thirds of Americans had personally donated to the March of Dimes. This was everyone's fight and victory seemed close at hand.

Field Trials

Beginning on April 26, 1954, nearly 1.8 million children participated in the field trial of Jonas Salk's killed-virus vaccine. The vaccines used in the field trials were triple tested for safety and potency by the drug manufacturer, Salk's laboratory, and the Public Health Service. The children who lined up and rolled up their sleeves were called Polio Pioneers. Each child got a special pin and a lollypop as a reward for their service to medicine.

Over the course of the experiment, some children received three injections of the vaccine. Others received three injections of a salt solution. This was the placebo, a harmless substance that looks like the real vaccine, but is inert. Still other children were an observed control group, meaning they did not receive the vaccine or the placebo, but were given regular health checks and blood tests to determine how many unvaccinated people might contract polio in a given area.

Neither the medical staff who performed the injections nor the children who received them knew whether they were getting the vaccine or the placebo. This type of experiment is called a double-blind trial, and it helps ensure that people's biases and expectations don't corrupt the results of the scientific experiment.

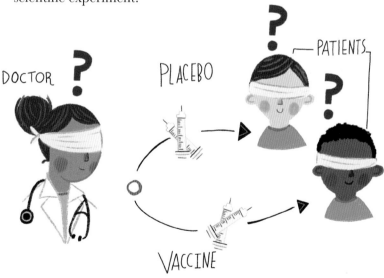

DOCTOR

PLACEBO

PATIENTS

VACCINE

Salk had protested the idea of a placebo group. He wanted everyone to receive the life-protecting shot. But he ultimately trusted the advice of his old mentor Dr. Francis, who supervised the trial and analyzed the data. Francis persuaded him that this was the best way to produce measurable results that the scientific community needed to approve the vaccine for public use.

Dr. Francis and a large staff of statisticians, many of whom usually worked for the US Census Bureau, collected and analyzed the data. Remember that this was well before the internet or the use of personal computers, so each of the 1.8 million participants had a paper file filled with forms and test results. Collecting and interpreting the data took Francis and his team nearly a year. During that time, he refused to tell Salk, O'Conner, or anyone else at NFIP how the results were shaping up. He wanted to understand every aspect of the results before he gave any reports.

Salk returned to his lab with nervous energy. He and his team continued to test and perfect new versions of the vaccine. O'Conner was so confident in the trials that he had vaccine manufacturers produce nine million doses of the vaccine. He wanted them to be ready to ship immediately when the results proved what he already believed: the vaccine was safe and effective.

Can You Patent the Sun?

On April 12, 1955, in a ballroom on the campus of the University of Michigan in Ann Arbor, over 150 reporters crowded around a stage, impatient for information. Around the country, teachers, students, office workers, factory workers, mothers, and fathers huddled around their radios and television sets and held their breath. This was the ten-year anniversary of Franklin Delano Roosevelt's death and the culmination of three decades of fundraising, research, and hope in the face of the nation's most dreaded disease. Everyone was ready for a breakthrough.

Agents from the university's press office were supposed to hand out paper copies of the vaccine trial results in an orderly fashion at 9:10 a.m. sharp, but they arrived a few minutes late and were mobbed by reporters. To protect themselves from the riotous rush, the university press agents scrambled onto a table, ripped open the boxes of neatly printed reports, and hurled them into the crowd.

By 9:20 a.m., the word was out: the field trials, the most massive medical test in American history, were a success. Dr. Francis reported that the vaccine was 60 percent to 70 percent effective in protecting against paralytic polio and 70 percent to 90 percent effective against all other types of polio. In other words, Jonas Salk's killed-virus vaccine did exactly what he said it would do. It protected people from the deadly disease

that had paralyzed the nation, both mentally and physically, for over a half century.

Church bells rang. Car horns honked. Factory whistles blew. School children cheered and threw their schoolwork into the air. Around the country, people hugged and cried and danced in the streets. Kids would be safer. Families wouldn't have to live in fear of summer or swimming pools or sudden plagues of paralysis. Humanity finally had a weapon in the crusade against poliomyelitis.

On a national television program that night, Edward R. Murrow, one of America's most trusted news anchors, interviewed Jonas Salk. He asked Salk, "Who owns the patent on this vaccine?" Meaning, who would receive the profits from selling the vaccine? Salk replied, "Well, the people, I would say. There is no patent. Could you patent the sun?"

Salk's polio vaccine belonged to everyone.

The Continuing Fight Against Polio

The NFIP immediately coordinated mass vaccination campaigns across the United States. Several other countries followed suit. Polio cases in the United States dropped from thirty-five thousand in 1955 to five thousand six hundred cases in 1957. By 1961, the country reported under one thousand cases.

Jonas Salk was praised as a national hero and became the face of scientific achievement. He received a Presidential Citation from Dwight D. Eisenhower in 1955 and a Presidential Medal of Freedom from Jimmy Carter in 1977.

Although the public loved him, the scientific community never accepted Jonas Salk as one of its own. Albert Sabin continued to downplay the success of the Salk vaccine while he continued to work on his own. When his live-virus oral vaccine was finally ready for large-scale human trials in 1957, he found few people in the United States interested in testing it. They were happy with Salk's vaccine. So Sabin partnered with researchers in Mexico and the Soviet Union to conduct his field trials. In Russia, researchers used his oral vaccine to inoculate eight million children against polio. It proved a success.

The Sabin vaccine was cheaper and easier to produce than Salk's. And because it was an oral vaccine, it was easier for children to take. It could even be placed on a sugar cube. Millions of doses were shipped all over the world, and by the end of the 1960s, it was the predominant polio vaccine used in the United States. Like Salk, Sabin refused to patent his vaccine so that it would remain affordable and available to everyone.

By 1979, polio was declared eradicated in the United States, and by 1994, the WHO declared it eradicated in the western hemisphere. But polio still exists, popping up in other countries from time to time, which is why the polio vaccine is still part of the standard series of vaccines recommended for all children.

In 1999, the United States switched back to Salk's killed-virus vaccine as the standard polio vaccine and it is still used today. It had been determined to be the safest option because of the extremely slight risk of live-virus vaccines giving someone an actual polio infection. Sabin's live-virus oral vaccine is still widely used in ongoing global campaigns to eradicate polio once and for all.

CHAPTER 9

MAURICE HiLLEMAN AND THE QUEST TO END CHiLDHOOD SUFFERiNG

If the first half of the twentieth century was an age of scientific discovery, the second half was an age of scientific refinement. Even though vaccines had saved millions of lives, there were still problems with the manufacturing process. It could be difficult to produce enough vaccines, and on rare occasions, a vaccine could be tainted with an impurity that did more harm than good when administered to the patient.

The yellow fever vaccine that saved the lives of thousands

of people also gave some people hepatitis because the serum (blood) used to make it contained the hepatitis virus. The rabies vaccine sometimes caused a life-threatening auto-immune response. When the cowpox material used to create the smallpox vaccine was collected "arm to arm," meaning it was taken from an infected person's arm and used directly in another person, it could carry a variety of diseases.

Other problems were those of scale. Brilliant research-ers might be able to isolate a virus and create a prototype vaccine, but they didn't have the means to produce millions of doses. Even Jonas Salk's polio vaccine was complicated to reproduce. In April 1955, a batch of polio vaccines pro-duced by Cutter Laboratories was not fully inactivated and tragically contained live polio virus. This mistake caused forty thousand cases of polio, one of the worst disasters in American medical history. But the Cutter incident led to an increased emphasis on vaccine safety, purity, and oversight.

While medical researchers had made huge strides in understanding and improving immunity, they were still per-fecting the mechanisms needed to provide vaccines to the world. One man would emerge as a champion of vaccine safety. He would also make it his life's goal to end childhood suffering. His name was Maurice Hilleman.

Maurice Hilleman in Montana

Maurice Hilleman's childhood was anything but easy. He started life during the worst pandemic in recorded history, the Spanish flu. Tragedy marked him on the day he was born, August 30, 1919, in Miles City, Montana. His twin sister was stillborn. His mother died two days later from a medical condition that effects pregnant women. Maurice, the only survivor of the traumatic birth, was the youngest of eight children and was given to his aunt and uncle who lived next door. This created one of the driving desires of his life: to prove to his biological father that he was worthy.

The separation also set young Maurice against his father's beliefs. While his father was a devout Lutheran and therefore did not believe in evolution, Maurice spent church services reading Charles Darwin's *On the Origin of Species* and learning everything he could about evolution. His aunt and uncle encouraged him to be a free thinker, to question and explore. He was fascinated with science, but he still had to pitch in on the family farm alongside his siblings to help his family survive the Great Depression. Maurice worked on everything: fixing farm equipment; making brooms; pumping water; and growing, picking, and selling produce. He also worked in his family's business doing landscaping and tree surgery and selling flowers in town. But the chore that would serve him best later in life was tending to the family's flock of chickens. Maurice would feed and water the chickens, collect their eggs, and shovel and clean the droppings out of the chicken coops.

THE CHICKEN AND THE EGG

In 1931, Alice Woodruff and Ernest Goodpasture discovered that they could grow the fowlpox virus in chicken eggs. The researchers bathed eggs in alcohol and then set them on fire to sterilize the shell. Then they sliced a small window into the shell to insert the virus.

Chicken eggs proved to be an ideal environment for growing viruses because they were cheap, readily available, and provided a sterile, bacteria-free growth medium. Best of all, when researchers injected a virus into an egg, the virus treated the egg like one gigantic cell and reproduced like crazy.

Although Woodruff and Goodpasture didn't know it at the time, their findings would enable Maurice Hilleman and other vaccine makers to save millions of lives.

By the time he was a teenager, Maurice Hilleman had survived everything life on the plains could throw at him. He had nearly drowned in the Yellowstone River, nearly been hit by a freight train, and nearly suffocated from a severe diphtheria infection. But he endured his Montana childhood, graduated high school, and received a full scholarship to Montana State University, where he majored in chemistry and microbiology, graduating first in his class.

Maurice couldn't afford to go to medical school, so he applied for and received a full scholarship to the University of Chicago in 1941. He still didn't have any money, so he survived on one meal a day and slept in a room infested with bedbugs. But his real life was in the lab, and he soon made his first medical breakthrough. He studied a sexually transmitted disease called chlamydia, which can infect both men and women and lead to infertility in women. At the time, most medical professionals believed the disease was an untreatable virus, but Hilleman's research showed that it was actually a bacterium that only reproduced inside cells. Because of his findings, doctors realized they could use antibiotics to cure chlamydia infections and avoid the long-term damage it caused to reproductive health.

Hilleman graduated from the University of Chicago in 1944. His professors expected him to begin a proper profession as a medical researcher or a professor. But he was still a self-described "cowboy" from Montana, and he still didn't like being told what to do. Hilleman wanted to do more than research; he wanted to help people. In the 1940s there were still several diseases that could harm or kill a child. Some of those diseases could inflict permanent damage or death before a baby was even born. Hilleman was smart enough and stubborn enough to believe that he could create a vaccine to prevent every disease that could harm or kill children. He joined the pharmaceutical industry to do just that.

Using Cocktail Blenders to Make Vaccines

Maurice Hilleman's first job after graduate school was at the E.R. Squibb pharmaceutical company in New Jersey. He started his career just as the United States entered World War II. Like Jonas Salk and other microbiology experts, Hilleman was recruited to help protect the soldiers heading into battle. While Salk and his colleagues in the Francis Lab were working on an influenza vaccine for the European Front, Hilleman was tasked with producing a vaccine for JEV. The disease is transmitted by mosquitos and can cause fever, seizures, paralysis, swelling of the brain (encephalitis), and death in one-third of those infected. Another one-third suffer permanent brain damage. American military personnel serving in Asia had no natural immunity to the disease and were vulnerable to severe infection.

Hilleman had studied JEV at the University of Chicago and knew that he could grow the virus in mice and deactivate it with formaldehyde. He was aware of other international trials that proved the deactivated virus produced immunity. He convinced the military to give his company the contract, saying he could have his production facility cranking out the vaccine within thirty days. There was just one problem: His company didn't have any facilities ready to produce the vaccines. So Hilleman convinced the company to let him renovate a horse barn on the back of their property. He and an engineer drew up plans, bulldozed out the horse manure, painted the concrete floor, and turned the barn into a production facility.

In a matter of weeks, he had a team of lab technicians growing JEV in mice. Waring Blenders, popular home cocktail blenders at that time, mixed formaldehyde with the mouse JEV to kill every particle of the JEV virus inside the tissue and produce a safe and effective vaccine. Within three months, Hilleman's team made enough doses

of the vaccine to protect six hundred thousand soldiers from Japanese encephalitis, saving thousands of lives.

Hilleman vs. Influenza

Science doesn't just solve a problem, dust off its lab coat, and move on. The discipline continues working on a problem to find the best solution with the freshest data available. Researchers had created an influenza vaccine in 1942 and that vaccine worked…the first year. The second year, not so much. Maurice Hilleman was the first person to figure out why.

Hilleman discovered and described the mechanisms of antigenic drift and antigenic shift in the 1940s. This is the process by which a virus's surface proteins mutate gradually (drift) or suddenly (shift) to avoid detection by the host's immune system. Hilleman studied the waning effectiveness of the first influenza vaccines and realized that vaccines would have to change from year to year to meet the threat of the mutating virus. Vaccine makers were able to use this information to improve the effectiveness of influenza vaccines by constantly updating them with new viral strains. Even today, the biggest challenge in creating flu vaccines is deciding which strains of influenza will become the most dangerous. The yearly influenza vaccines usually contain three to four viral strains that represent a best guess at the viruses that have the potential to do the most harm. These strains are voted on twice a year by an international body of researchers who monitor influenza in animal and human hosts around the world. This necessary and life-saving process can be traced back to Hilleman.

In 1957, Maurice Hilleman used his vast knowledge of epidemiology and virology to do something no one had ever done before: He predicted a flu pandemic. At the time, Hilleman was working for Walter Reed Institute in Washington, DC, as the head of the central laboratory for the military worldwide surveillance for early detection of pandemic viruses. He collaborated on surveillance with the WHO, which had formed as a branch of the United Nations after World War II.

That year, Hilleman discovered warning signs of a coming pandemic not in the blood samples of service person-nel but in the pages of the *New York Times*. On April 17, 1957, the newspaper ran an article titled "Hong Kong Battling Influenza Epidemic." The article noted that two hundred fifty thousand people had been infected so far and said that local authorities were calling it the "worst epidemic outbreak in years." The short article, which amounted to four small paragraphs tucked onto the third page of the newspaper, ended with the haunting description, "thousands of sick persons have stood in long lines awaiting treatment in clinics. Many women carried glassy-eyed children tied to their backs."

Hilleman recounted that when he finished reading the article, he put down the paper and said, "My God! This is the pandemic. It's here."

This influenza virus had the potential to become the pandemic the world had been dreading since the Spanish flu disappeared in 1920. Hilleman contacted a US Army laboratory in Japan to investigate. The medical officer located a navy crewman who had contracted the virus in Hong Kong. The officer had the man gargle and spit into a cup and then quickly sent the sample to Hilleman. He received the sample on May 17, one month after reading the *New York Times* article.

Hilleman was able to isolate the virus. He carefully grew the virus in a chicken egg and then tested it in the blood samples of hundreds of military personnel and civilians. Not one person Hilleman tested had any natural immunity to this strain of influenza. He sent virus samples to colleagues around the world and found that only a small group of elderly people had any immunity: seventy- and eighty-year-olds who had been infected by—and survived—a deadly influenza pandemic from 1889 to 1890. That pandemic had killed an estimated six million people worldwide. Hilleman calculated that the pandemic would hit America by September, just as school children were returning from summer break. He knew that if this virus was allowed to spread across the globe and through crowded classrooms the results would be catastrophic.

He raised the alarm in an urgent press release, but most medical professionals in the United States and around the world didn't believe him. He sent the samples to Thomas

Francis, Jonas Salk's mentor at the University of Michigan. Francis was now the head of the Influenza Commission for the American military. Francis, too, ignored the warning and said that he didn't see a need to create a vaccine. Finally, Maurice Hilleman parked himself in the entrance of Francis's favorite restaurant and ambushed the doctor when he arrived for dinner. Hilleman told one of the most respected influenza researchers in the world that he was making a huge mistake by ignoring the virus. If Hilleman was wrong, a move like this could cost him his career. But he managed to convince Dr. Francis to look at his evidence, and finally, Francis agreed.

This was an alarming strain with pandemic potential, and the entire world was in its crosshairs.

From there, Maurice Hilleman called in favors with friends at pharmaceutical companies across the country. He enlisted six companies to produce the vaccine. He wanted to make sure as many people as possible could get vaccinated before kids returned to classrooms and the fall flu season started. One thing was certain: Eggs would play a critical role in vaccine production. Roughly speaking, one chicken egg produces one dose of a vaccine. Hilleman knew vaccine production inside and out. He also grew up farming chickens, so he knew that farmers would have to spare all the roosters they could so companies would have enough fertilized eggs to make the vaccines. With the egg problem solved, the companies would have about four months to produce as many influenza vaccines as possible.

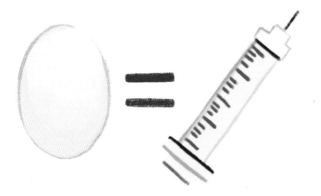

The vaccination rollout started in July, and by late fall, the United States was able to vaccinate forty million people against Asian influenza. And the influenza did become a pandemic. As Hilleman had forecast, the virus struck America in September of 1957. The first cases were brought by navy crews to bases on the east and west coasts. From there, the wave of influenza quickly spread across the country. Luckily, many millions of Americans had acquired immunity through Hilleman's vaccine.

In all, the 1957 influenza killed seventy thousand Americans and four million people internationally. But without Hilleman's efforts, the death toll could have been much higher. For vaccinating millions of people and saving thousands of lives, Hilleman was awarded the military's Distinguished Service Medal. To this day, he is the only person to successfully predict a pandemic and to rush a vaccine out in time to protect people against it.

The Jeryl Lynn Strain

Some researchers search the world for the perfect strain of virus to use in a vaccine. Others find it closer to home. For Maurice Hilleman, the perfect strain of the mumps virus was a little too close to home. It infected his five-year-old daughter in 1963.

Mumps is a viral infection that causes fever, aches, and swelling of the salivary glands just in front of the ears. People with mumps are often described as having chipmunk cheeks because of their swollen glands. While most people with mumps recover, the virus can also cause permanent damage and death. Before the vaccine, mumps was the leading cause of childhood meningitis, a swelling of the lining of the brain and spinal cord. Mumps can also cause orchitis (an infection and swelling of the testicles) in up to one-third of infected males, which can leave them unable to father children. A mumps infection during pregnancy can cause the death of the unborn child.

When Hilleman's daughter, Jeryl Lynn, came into his room in the middle of the night to say she wasn't feeling well, he felt her neck, consulted his medical guide, and realized she was suffering from mumps. He tucked her back into bed, then jumped into his car and drove to his lab to retrieve cotton swabs and nutrient broth. When he got home, he woke up Jeryl Lynn, swabbed her throat gently, and then returned to the lab with the sample of her virus. Jeryl Lynn made a full recovery, and Hilleman had a fresh sample of mumps virus for his experiments.

Over the next two years, Hilleman passed his daughter's mumps through a series of chicken eggs and chicken cell cultures to attenuate the strain. The virus mutated slightly to become better and better at infecting and destroying chicken cells, but those adaptations made it worse and worse at infecting human cells.

When Hilleman determined the virus was weak enough, he recruited doctors Robert Weibel and Joseph Stokes Jr. to test the vaccine in children in and around Philadelphia. Two hundred children received the vaccine and two hundred received the placebo. Soon after, a mumps outbreak spread throughout the city. Only two of the children who received the vaccine

got sick compared to sixty-one children who received the placebo. The vaccine was a success. It was officially licensed just four years after Jeryl Lynn Hilleman's original illness.

To honor her contribution to global health, Maurice Hilleman named the mumps vaccine after his daughter. If you have been vaccinated for the mumps, you received the Jeryl Lynn strain. Her 1963 infection has kept you and millions of others safe.

Too Toxic

While he was developing the mumps vaccine, Hilleman was also hard at work on a measles vaccine. In the 1960s, measles was one of those childhood viruses that most people caught.

While some people saw it as a childhood rite of passage that was no big deal, the disease actually killed about eight million children a year worldwide. Measles is one of the most highly infectious diseases known to humankind. It spreads through aerosolized respiratory droplets that a sick person expels through breathing, laughing, coughing, and sneezing. After leaving the body of a host, the viral droplets remain active in the air and can infect people for several hours.

The measles infection starts with a fever, runny nose, pink eye, and a rash that begins at the hairline and spreads across the victim's entire body. Most people recover in a few weeks, but about three in every ten infections lead to serious complications: ear infections, deafness, pneumonia, encephalitis, seizures, brain damage, hemorrhaging underneath the skin, blindness, and long-term damage to the heart, liver, and kidneys. Tragically, some children who seem to recover from measles can develop subacute sclerosing panencephalitis (SSPE) up to seven years after the initial infection. SSPE causes a slow deterioration of the brain and is always fatal.

Maurice Hilleman was passionate about finding a cure for the disease, but this time he didn't get the strain from his daughter. The measles virus he worked with came from a thirteen-year-old boy named David Edmonston who caught the virus while attending a boys' private school outside of Boston in 1954. Thomas Peebles, a member of John Enders's

ROALD DAHL'S DAUGHTER OLIVIA

In 1962, famous children's author Roald Dahl lost his seven-year-old daughter Olivia to a measles infection that developed into encephalitis. He dedicated his book *James and the Giant Peach* to Olivia while she was alive and *The BFG* to her memory. Roald Dahl became a passionate supporter of vaccines and pleaded with parents to protect their children from vaccine-preventable diseases, like measles.

laboratory at Boston Children's Hospital, collected samples of the strain.

John Enders and his team had recently won the 1954 Nobel Prize in Physiology or Medicine for their technique for growing poliomyelitis in cell cultures. Enders and Peebles spent six years passing the Edmonston strain of measles through a variety of cells. They were trying to attenuate the virus to the point where it could induce immunity without making people sick.

They tested their version of the vaccine on children in 1958 and 1960. In both tests, the vaccine prevented a full-blown measles infection, but it also had a high rate of side effects, including rash and fever. Some children had fevers that were so high they caused seizures.

Enders sent his lab's findings and attenuated measles strain to Maurice Hilleman to begin mass producing a vaccine. Hilleman conducted more tests on the attenuated strain and declared that it was much too toxic.

In addition to the negative side effects it caused, the Enders vaccine had also been created in eggs that contained a chicken leukemia virus, which caused cancerous tumors and death in chickens. Although the virus was later determined to be harmless to humans, Hilleman refused to take chances. He rejected the idea of mass producing the Enders vaccine in its original form. Instead, he chose to redesign the vaccine.

He again worked with Joseph Stokes Jr., who had helped him test the mumps vaccine. Stokes was an expert in gamma globulin, the part of blood that contains antibodies. In the 1930s, Stokes had shown that people treated with gamma globulin from polio survivors were protected from polio infections. Stokes suggested that combining an injection of the measles vaccine and an injection of gamma globulin would mitigate the side effects of the vaccine. The idea worked.

Next Hilleman had to tackle the chicken leukemia virus. He had to find a flock of birds that had no trace of the virus. There was only one such flock in the country: at Kimber Farms in Fremont, California. Kimber Farms specialized in combining genetics and farming. Since the 1930s, its employees had been working to selectively breed disease-free eggs and disease-resistant chickens. They took eggs from disease-free chickens, dipped those eggs in iodine, and then hatched them in incubators. They also kept their research flock in facilities that were placed away from and up-wind of other chicken populations. The facilities had screens to keep out flies and rodents that might transmit disease. Anyone who entered the facility had to wear protective clothing and even disinfect their shoes to avoid tracking in germs. Hilleman needed those chickens.

When he flew to California to try to buy the chickens, both the principal investigator and the director of poultry research refused to sell even a few birds. But Hilleman noticed that the director had a familiar accent. He asked the man where he was from. The man told him Helena, Montana. Hilleman told him he was from Miles City, Montana. The director shook Hilleman's hand and agreed to sell him the entire research flock for a dollar a bird.

Hilleman released his redeveloped, chicken-leukemia-free version of the Enders measles vaccine in 1963. His vaccine saved thousands of lives. But Hilleman was not fully satisfied, because the vaccine had to be given with an injection of gamma globulin. Two shots. One vaccine.

So Hilleman kept tinkering. He took the Enders vaccine and passed it through chicken embryo cells forty more times to create what he called the More Attenuated Enders strain, or the Moraten strain. This version of the vaccine was attenuated to the point that it no longer caused side effects and no longer required an additional shot of gamma globulin. Hilleman's improved measles vaccine was released in 1968 and has been the only measles vaccine used in the United States ever since. Measles cases in the United States have decreased from four million infections a year to fewer than fifty cases. Hilleman, his

team, and his chickens had effectively stopped the spread of one of the world's most infectious diseases.

Reducing Suffering

Hilleman and peers like Jonas Salk had been so successful at creating vaccines to end childhood disease that they had inadvertently created a new form of childhood suffering: too many

shots. Yes, the shots staved off much worse pains and danger, but they still added up to a lot of needles and a lot of baby tears. In the late 1960s, Hilleman started working on a single shot that combined his mumps and measles vaccines with the vaccine for rubella.

Rubella, also known as German measles, is an infection in children that causes a mild fever, swollen glands, sore joints, and a rash across the face. Nearly all children who are infected recover from rubella. The real danger of the virus is its impact on unborn children. If a pregnant person is infected with rubella early in the pregnancy, the fetus will die or develop permanent birth defects 85 percent of the time.

Before there were reliable vaccines, young girls were sent to rubella parties to purposely catch and recover from the virus before they reached their childbearing years. In the 1960s, a series of rubella epidemics swept the United States. The 1963–1964 epidemic claimed the lives of eight thousand babies.

Maurice Hilleman had started working on his own rubella vaccine when another vaccine created by a researcher named

Harry Meyer beat his to the testing phase. Hilleman was driven by results rather than ego, so, in the interest of releasing a much-needed vaccine as soon as possible, he abandoned his vaccine to improve and release Meyer's vaccine first.

Another medical researcher, Stanley Plotkin, eventually released an even better rubella vaccine. As a physician, Plotkin had cared for hundreds of women whose pregnancies had been affected by the rubella epidemics. He had seen first-hand how devastating the virus could be. He attenuated his vaccine in cells from a human cell line, making it free of any animal viruses that might cause harm.

When Hilleman recognized that Plotkin's rubella vaccine was safer and more effective than Meyer's vaccine, he called Plotkin and asked to produce his vaccine.

In 1971, Hilleman completed and released his shot that combined the vaccines for mumps, measles, and rubella. That shot became known as the MMR. Not only did the MMR reduce the number of shots young children received and the number of tears children shed, it also enabled medical field workers around the world to quickly vaccinate millions of children in remote areas of the globe, saving countless young lives.

Preventing Cancer, One Shot at a Time

Maurice Hilleman had accomplished many things in the fight against infectious diseases, but he knew he still had a debt to repay to his oldest friend from his Montana childhood: the chicken. He told an interviewer, "Chickens were my best friends. They helped me so much. Maybe I could do something for them."

Growing up on the farm, Hilleman knew the problems that chicken sicknesses could cause. Viruses could sweep through a flock causing everything from cancerous tumors to chicken leukemia. His family couldn't eat, sell, or trade sick chickens. One of the most common chicken illnesses was Marek's disease, which attacked a chicken's nerves, causing paralysis and eventually tumors throughout all major organs.

The disease was caused by a type of herpesvirus. In the 1960s, a poultry center isolated the virus and gave its sample to Hilleman. He was able to attenuate the virus and create a vaccine to give to day-old chicks. The vaccine prevented the virus and the cancer it caused, saving millions of chickens' lives. Before the vaccine, chicken had been a more expensive type of meat, something families ate only on special occasions and holidays. Hilleman's vaccine made chicken and eggs affordable food products and revolutionized the poultry industry.

Hilleman's contribution to cancer treatments didn't stop with chickens. He also furthered the field of research around interferons, proteins that your body creates when it fights a viral infection. Interferons are part of your natural defenses. They tell your immune system that germs or cancer cells are in your body, triggering killer immune cells to fight the invaders. They "interfere" with viruses, keeping them from multiplying.

Hilleman was the first person to purify, describe, and mass-produce interferons. He discovered that these proteins inhibited the growth of viruses and prevented cancers caused by viruses. His work led to the use of interferons in treating chronic viral infections and to some cancer treatments.

Hilleman also created a vaccine to prevent hepatitis B, which is the world's leading cause of liver disease and liver cancer, the third-most-common type of cancer. To make his vaccine, he collected blood samples from people who had the infection, including drug users. Then he created a new system to deactivate any and all viruses in the blood. He tested his deactivation process on every known virus to ensure that no live virus would be able to infect people through the vaccine.

He said the process would render all viruses "deader than deader than dead." His safe and effective hepatitis B vaccine hit the market in 1981, right around the time doctors and scientists were beginning to document an emerging disease that could be transmitted through blood, human immunodeficiency virus (HIV)—the virus that causes acquired immuno- deficiency syndrome (AIDS).

One of the hallmarks of a great scientist is their ability to change their mind in light of new information. Hilleman knew that he had a safe and effective vaccine against hepatitis B. He knew that his method of deactivation would kill any virus, including HIV. But he also realized that people were too scared to take the vaccine because it had been made using the blood of individuals who were more at risk for having HIV: drug users. Ultimately, he decided to redevelop the vaccine.

Hilleman looked to a relatively new medical technology called recombinant DNA technology, or genetic engineering. Geneticists were able to grow hepatitis B surface proteins in yeast so the proteins would not have to be sourced from human blood. Hilleman's new and improved vaccine for hepatitis B, the first vaccine ever to use recombinant DNA technology, was available in 1986. Since then, the rate of hepatitis B for children and teenagers in the United States has decreased by 95 percent. Experts estimate that the vaccine could eliminate liver cancer in the next twenty to thirty years.

Hilleman's revolutionary use of genetically engineered proteins also paved the way for a new generation of safe and effective vaccines, such as the vaccine against human papillomavirus (HPV), a virus that can cause cervical cancer.

Hilleman's Legacy

Maurice Hilleman wasn't a man who rested on his laurels or spent much time celebrating his successes. He didn't seek out fame or television cameras to capitalize on his work. He was too busy doing his job. The work ethic etched into him during the Great Depression on his family's Montana farm was forever in his thoughts. When he reflected on his life, Hilleman said his plan was always to be "doing something useful and being useful to the world."

Hilleman's colleagues and family have noted that he constantly carried a list of diseases in his pocket. These were the diseases that he had yet to conquer. When he finished one vaccine, he'd consult his list and get working on the next disease in line. He was relentless in his mission to protect babies and children from needless suffering and death.

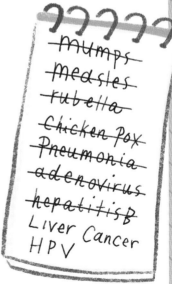

By the end of his career, Maurice Hilleman had created forty vaccines to prevent a host of devastating diseases, including mumps, measles, rubella, chicken pox, pneumonia, adenovirus, and hepatitis B. He developed nine of the fourteen vaccines currently recommended as essential for all US children. He was the first person to create a vaccine against cancer, first in chickens and then in humans. He is still the only person to ever successfully predict an influenza pandemic. Experts estimate that his work saves the lives of eight million children each year and has increased the average American life span by thirty years.

When Maurice Hilleman passed away in 2005, the world was in desperate need of a new master vaccine maker.

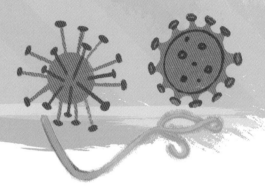

CHAPTER 10

AN AGE OF PANDEMICS

While 2019 marked humanity's first deadly encounter with COVID-19, it wasn't our first tango with a novel virus or even our first pandemic scare of the twenty-first century. In fact, new viruses with the potential to cause a global pandemic have emerged at an alarming rate in recent years. Since the WHO created its pandemic warning system in 2005, it has issued six declarations of a Public Health Emergency of International Concern (PHEIC) in fifteen years. The WHO defines a PHEIC as "an extraordinary event which is determined to constitute a public health risk to other States through the international spread of disease and to potentially require a coordinated international response."

Experts theorize that the accelerated pace of emerging diseases with pandemic potential stems from humanity's continuing push into natural habitats. The rise of civilization has always coincided with the rise of infectious disease. As the human population continues to grow, people encroach farther and farther into animal habitats. As people cut down forests to create farmland, they displace or hunt and eat animals that they didn't used to encounter in the wild. Farming also brings domesticated animals like pigs and chickens into

contact with wild animals, causing an opportunity for diseases to mix together in vessels like pigs and then jump to humans. Additionally, human and animal waste creates new strain on the delicate balance of water and soil.

Climate change has the potential to spread new viruses as animals lose their habitats to rising temperatures and sea levels. Warmer weather is also releasing diseases like anthrax that had been frozen in permafrost in areas like Siberia. Scientists worry that even older bacteria and viruses could emerge from thawing permafrost causing a reawakening of diseases that human immune systems haven't had to fight for hundreds or even thousands of years.

Here's a look at some recent viruses that have kept epidemiologists up at night. Although there are other emerging viruses for which vaccines have not been created, these are the viruses for which scientists have developed effective vaccines.

Ebola

Ebola is a hemorrhagic fever, which causes massive internal and external bleeding. It was first identified in the Democratic Republic of Congo (formerly Zaire) in 1976. Researchers believe that population growth and settlement into previously wild areas caused the disease to jump from fruit bats to gorillas, chimpanzees, and humans. Humans can catch the disease directly from infected animals, often by hunting bush meat.

The disease can also pass from human to human when people come into contact with infected blood.

Outbreaks have spread across Africa since the 1970s. One of the most recent outbreaks, the 2014–2015 West Africa outbreak, prompted the WHO to issue a declaration of a PHEIC. Ebola kills about 50 percent of people who are infected. After nearly four decades and twenty-five deadly outbreaks, researchers were able to develop a vaccine. Health workers use a strategy called ring vaccination to identify and vaccinate people who might have encountered an infected individual. The vaccinations cut off transmission routes for the virus. The United States and other countries have a strategic stockpile of Ebola vaccines in case a pandemic emerges.

Avian Flu (H5N1)

In 1997, a young boy in Hong Kong played with a baby chick at daycare. He died six days later of a disease that caused organ failure. He was the first known victim of avian flu. The disease is caused by the H5N1 influenza strain and usually only infects birds. Most influenza that jumps from animals to humans first moves through pigs and mixes with human virus strains. H5N1 jumped directly from birds to humans, something that scientists hadn't believed was possible. Since then, the virus has continued to spread around the globe through wild bird populations. Sometimes farmers can't even tell their chickens are sick until they flop over, dead.

Although H5N1 rarely infects humans and it can't yet move from one human to another, the virus has a death rate of 60 percent in humans. It also causes outbreaks in domesticated animals like cats, dogs, pigs, ferrets, and birds. The disease jumped to tigers at the Sriracha Tiger Zoo in Bangkok in 2004. The tigers had been infected by eating raw chicken that contained the virus. H5N1 also spread directly from tiger to tiger causing the deaths of nearly one hundred and fifty tigers before zookeepers contained the spread.

There is a widely available H5N1 vaccine…for poultry. Agriculture agencies and public health experts work to monitor the virus in domesticated and wild flocks and move quickly to destroy infected flocks as soon as possible when the virus appears. Researchers have also created human vaccines. Some are still in experimental phases. Others are reserved for non-civilian use and kept in military stockpiles. These vaccines would not protect the global population from potential viral mutations. Influenza experts fear that if H5N1 mutates so that it can spread directly from person to person, the death toll would rival that of the 1918 pandemic.

Swine Flu (H1N1)

In 2009, a highly transmittable strain of influenza circled the globe. Scientists realized that it was H1N1, a version of the strain that had caused the 1918 pandemic and had killed fifty to one hundred million people. The 2009 virus is called H1N1pdm09. It emerged in California in April. The viral strain was a reassortment of bird and human influenza mixed with two different strains of swine flu. While some of the infected people had been around pigs, others had been infected by human-to-human spread. By June, the WHO declared swine flu a global pandemic. By October, forty-nine out of fifty states reported widespread instances of the disease. Swine flu mainly infected children and young adults, while many people over sixty seemed to have immunity from a previous influenza outbreak. By the start of the fall flu season, the US Food and Drug Administration (FDA) approved six vaccines against swine flu and had called for increased production of antiviral medications to help people who were already infected. The WHO declared the end of the pandemic in August 2010.

During the pandemic, the disease infected an estimated 11 to 21 percent of the world's population and caused about 284,000 deaths. Swine flu is now endemic, meaning it circulates through the population as part of the seasonal flu. Although it hasn't reached the infection levels it caused in 2009, swine flu is still responsible for a high number of infections and deaths every year.

Rumors of a New Plague: SARS-CoV-2

January 2020 was a time of great uncertainty. Whispers of a new virus in China trickled into the news cycle. At first the illness seemed like a minor concern happening a world away, but more and more people throughout China and then Asia fell ill with the mysterious disease. Rumors spread that countries around the world might scale back sporting events and concerts or even close airports. But the idea of a large-scale disruption of life as we know it was unthinkable.

By February, people carried mini bottles of hand sanitizer and wondered if it was still safe to shake hands and started quietly buying extra rolls of toilet paper…just in case.

By March, government-mandated lockdowns forced people into their homes for their own safety. Grocery store workers became essential workers, heroes who kept doing their jobs while many people worked from home. Deer roamed through quiet city streets. Dolphins swam in the deserted canals of Venice. Much of the world was quarantined in an attempt to "flatten the curve," meaning reduce transmissions and hospitalizations related to a virus that was now causing a full-blown pandemic.

One question swirled through everyone's mind: "When will the pandemic end?" Medical experts around the world answered: "When we create a vaccine."

Maurice Hilleman had held the record for the quickest development of a vaccine for his work on mumps: four years. Medical research and technology has improved since then, but those improvements don't always equate to a reduced timeline for innovation.

But humanity's clock was ticking. The world couldn't wait even four years for a vaccine. We needed a new and ingenious method for fighting a new and terrifying disease.

CHAPTER 11

COViD-19

We don't yet know the exact origin of the deadliest pandemic in a century.

The official name for the virus is SARS-CoV-2, which stands for Severe Acute Respiratory Syndrome-Corona Virus–2. It comes from a family of coronaviruses that often infect animals and humans. The first human coronavirus was discovered and described by June Almeida in 1964. Almeida was an expert in identifying and photographing viruses. Using an electron microscope, she was able to see the virus

in great detail, right down to the proteins that protrude off its surface like the spikes of a crown. She and her colleagues called the virus a coronavirus because *corona* is the Latin word for "crown."

Researchers have since identified seven coronaviruses that can infect people. Some coronaviruses cause common colds. Others cause global pandemics.

SARS-CoV-2 causes the illness we commonly call COVID-19. One of the reasons it was able to spread so quickly and infect so many people is that this is a novel virus. While diseases like anthrax gained the ability to infect both animals and humans thousands of years ago, SARS-CoV-2 first mutated into a strain that can infect humans in fall 2019. No one on the planet had immunity to the disease. Additionally, no one knew what symptoms the disease would cause or how it would progress. People had been describing the progression of smallpox infections for nearly four thousand years before Edward Jenner created his vaccine against it, but COVID-19 was a mystery.

Medical experts studied the new virus, created tests to determine if people were infected, and identified the common symptoms and means of transmission. While experts first thought the virus spread more like the common cold and flu— through large respiratory droplets produced while coughing and sneezing—they soon realized that the virus acted much more like the highly infectious measles virus. COVID can linger in the air in tiny, aerosolized particles for up to three hours and remain infectious the entire time.

Once someone is exposed to COVID, symptoms usually begin in two to fourteen days. Some people, called asymptomatic carriers, might not have any symptoms at all but can still transmit the virus to others. Other carriers can spread the disease to others before they even realize they are sick.

COVID was originally considered a respiratory disease, but researchers soon found that it had the potential to spread to multiple body systems. Severe cases were eerily similar to deaths recorded during the 1918 flu pandemic. One of the culprits of severe COVID complications is the cytokine storm,

CRISPR: A New Technology...Three Billion Years in the Making

In the distant past, viruses evolved so that they had the ability to infect bacteria. But bacteria themselves evolved a clever system for remembering viruses that infected them. They store bits of the virus's genetic material so that the next time the virus invades, the bacterium recognizes it and fights back, using enzymes to chop the invader to pieces. Once bacteria acquire this immunity, they pass it on to all future generations. Researchers called this bacterial immune system **CRISPR**, or **C**lustered **R**egularly **I**nterspaced **S**hort **P**alindromic **R**epeats.

Scientists also discovered they could use CRISPR like a pair of scissors to edit or repair genetic information. In the fight against COVID-19, researchers harnessed CRISPR technology to develop rapid tests that could help health experts identify the infection and track the rate and spread of the disease.

In the future, medical researchers could use CRISPR to replace a genetic mutation that causes cancer or fix a birth defect before a baby is born. CRISPR could also revolutionize the future of vaccines by introducing a fragment of a virus's genetic material into a person's body so they can gain immunity without ever getting sick.

when a victim's own immune system overreacts to an infection and floods the body with immune cells. Rather than fighting the infection, the immune cells attack organs and blood vessels, as in the 1918 pandemic.

Some sufferers recover from mild COVID infections within a few weeks. However, an estimated 30 percent of people who are infected develop a condition called post-COVID, chronic COVID, or long-haul COVID, during which symptoms such as loss of taste and smell, brain fog, memory loss, and malaise can persist for weeks or months. The virus is still too new for us to know whether people will recover fully from post-COVID conditions.

Even COVID cases that are mild or asymptomatic can still cause long-term damage.

In the first two years of the pandemic COVID-19 claimed the lives of nearly 1 million Americans and killed over six million people worldwide.

The situation can seem overwhelming, but sometimes hope comes from unexpected places, like a little glass vial filled with tiny particles of RNA.

Messenger RNA Vaccines

On January 9, 2020, something remarkable happened. Chinese researchers publicly posted the complete genome of SARS-CoV-2 on the internet so that every scientist in the world could help them find a way to fight the new disease. Medical researchers around the globe got to work.

When Maurice Hilleman suspected the 1957 Hong Kong flu would become a pandemic, he had to wait a month to get his hands on a sample of the virus and then had to spend several more weeks trying to figure out its secrets. The secrets of the coronavirus were free for the taking.

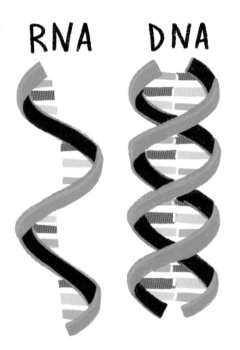

RNA   DNA

With the genetic sequence, two pharmaceutical companies were able to create vaccines in a matter of days. Others had vaccines ready within a few months. The key to this speed lies in the type of vaccine technology they used: messenger RNA (mRNA). If DNA is a complete user's manual your body needs to function, then RNA is the Post-it note that helps your cells remember short, specific instructions. RNA is a copy of a section of DNA. It tells the cell how to build essential proteins to carry out all functions of life as we know it.

SARS AND MERS CAUSE GLOBAL PANIC AND GREATER PREPAREDNESS

Louis Pasteur called rabies a virus just as Edward Jenner called cowpox a virus, but neither of them actually knew what a virus was. The word *virus* is from the Latin word for "poisonous secretion." Virus has been used since the fourteenth century to describe something that made people sick. Louis Pasteur could see and study bacteria through the microscopes of his time, but he couldn't see something as small as the microbes we now know as viruses.

In the 1890s, Russian botanist Dmitri Ivanovsky and Dutch microbiologist Martinus Beijerinck both separately theorized that something smaller than bacteria had to be infecting tobacco plants, but they still couldn't see or prove their theories. Scientists wouldn't prove the existence of viruses until Wendell Meredith Stanley invented the electron microscope in 1931. This was the first tool that allowed humans to see something as tiny as a virus.

The idea for mRNA vaccines has been around since the 1990s and researchers had even tried producing them during the SARS outbreak in the early 2000s. In 2005, Katalin Karikó and Drew Weissman from the University of Pennsylvania were the first researchers to prove that mRNA vaccines could be used in humans. Their work provided the basis for the vaccines in use today. In the United States, Moderna, Pfizer/BioNTech, and Johnson & Johnson were the first pharmaceutical companies to produce vaccines against COVID-19.

Past vaccines required years of attenuation to weaken a microbe or hundreds of chemical tests to deactivate it. Sometimes in the testing phase, vaccines would prove too weak to create an immune response or so strong that they caused the disease. Results like that would send researchers back to the drawing board. Some traditional vaccines also needed adjuvants, those extra ingredients required to stimulate the immune system to react to a vaccine. But adding adjuvants also means adding weeks of testing to make sure that the adjuvants themselves are safe and effective. None of these steps are necessary with mRNA vaccines.

Instead, researchers use mRNA to carry the instructions for making a piece of the SARS-CoV-2 spike protein. When the mRNA is injected into your arm, it enters your cells and teaches them to create and release this SARA-CoV-2 spike protein fragment. From there, your body's immune system takes over. It sees the spike protein as a foreign invader and produces antibodies to destroy it. If, in the future, your body is infected with the real virus, your immune system will recognize the virus's surface spike protein, remember how to fight it, and destroy the virus.

mRNA vaccines are safer to use than traditional vaccines because no part of the actual virus is ever injected into your body. You could never have a repeat of the Cutter incident, where several thousand people accidentally received vaccines containing live polio.

You also wouldn't run the risk of exposing yourself to a live virus in the lab. Unlike JEV or even Jeryl Lynn's mumps, the mRNA is harmless on its own. It's just a tiny set of instructions for making protein.

mRNA is also great to use in a vaccine because it works as its own adjuvant. Your body naturally identifies and destroys free-floating RNA because it serves no purpose outside of a cell and could be the leftover material from a cell that was destroyed by a virus. This means that the vaccines contain fewer ingredients and can be ready for testing faster.

Once researchers figured out how to edit the mRNA and how to keep the body from destroying it, they needed a way to deliver it into human cells. Vaccinologists at Moderna and Pfizer/BioNTech decided to use a technique that had been pioneered in the 1970s. They used Lipid Nano Particles (LNPs) as the delivery system. They're basically tiny balls of fat with mRNA inside. LNPs have the ability to stick to the membrane of human cells. Then the cell simply absorbs the LNP.

Johnson & Johnson uses mRNA technology in its vaccine, but it chose to deliver it into cells using a harmless virus. The virus acts like it always does in a host body; it finds a cell and injects genetic material. Only in this case, the genetic material is the mRNA code to create the spike fragment.

In extensive testing, the vaccines all proved safe and effective against COVID-19. In fact, after two doses of the Moderna and Pfizer/BioNTech's vaccines, both proved to be 90 percent to 95 percent effective in preventing infections. In comparison, annual flu vaccines are usually 40 percent to 60 percent effective against infection. Like flu 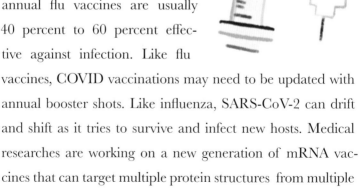 vaccines, COVID vaccinations may need to be updated with annual booster shots. Like influenza, SARS-CoV-2 can drift and shift as it tries to survive and infect new hosts. Medical researches are working on a new generation of mRNA vaccines that can target multiple protein structures from multiple variants to protect humans against all coronavirus variants.

A Dose of Hope

In December 2020, less than one year after Chinese researchers released the genetic code for SARS-CoV-2, the world had two safe and effective vaccines to offer protection from COVID-19. More vaccines would follow and the largest vaccination campaign in the history of the world began.

There was still work to be done to end the pandemic. Testing continued to ensure that the vaccines were safe for babies and children. Medical experts, community leaders, and friends had to convince hesitant people that the vaccine was the safest way to gain immunity against the virus. World leaders had to find ways to distribute vaccines in ways that were fair and equitable to all nations. We still have a long road ahead, but now, collectively, we also have something to celebrate.

On December 14, 2020, Sandra Lindsay, an Intensive Care Unit nurse at Long Island Jewish Medical Center in Queens, New York City, was one of the first people in the United States to receive the shot. She had been treating patients with severe complications from COVID-19 for months. Her healthcare system had treated over one hundred thousand COVID patients in the first year of the pandemic. After Lindsay received her vaccine, reporters asked her what the shot meant to her. She replied, "I feel like healing is coming."

CONCLUSION

....

The End of Smallpox

In 1967, the WHO, the United States, and the Soviet Union (now Russia) embarked on one of the most ambitious health projects ever undertaken. They were going to end transmission of smallpox once and for all. The disease had been eradicated in much of the world, but thirty-four countries around the world were still suffering from regular outbreaks that caused millions of deaths. Most of these outbreaks occurred in remote villages far from hospitals, clinics, or, in some cases, roads.

The United States and the Soviet Union donated a combined seventy-five million doses of the vaccine. That sounds like a lot of vaccines, but it wasn't nearly enough to put a shot in the arm of everyone on Earth who wasn't yet inoculated. Further complicating the efforts, the people who weren't vaccinated weren't going to line up at a hospital to let strangers inoculate them.

William Foege was Chief of the Smallpox Eradication Program for the Centers for Disease Control in Africa. He was also a Lutheran missionary doctor who spent much of his time in the field establishing trusting relationships with people in small villages. When he heard of a case of smallpox in a village, he and a team of healthcare workers immediately rushed to the area. He vaccinated the victim's family and anyone who might have had contact with them, but he didn't have enough doses of the vaccine for everyone in the region. He needed to be smart about tracking the disease and stopping it in its tracks.

Foege sent runners to nearby towns to identify other people who were infected. When they found someone, they again vaccinated the victim's family and anyone in close contact. They were building a barrier of human immunity around every victim they found so that smallpox would be cut off from future victims. They called this strategy ring immunity.

In the 1970s Dr. Larry Brilliant and his wife Girija were WHO public health experts working on the ring immunity program in India. He described the ring vaccination process

in his 2006 TED talk. "I got to see the last case of killer small-pox in the world," he told the audience.

They created a human network of surveillance. They gave out rewards for people who helped them find infected individuals. Whenever they identified a case, they inoculated everyone in the area, creating another ring of immunity. They repeated the process for years, hunting down every suspected case, penning in the virus, and using vaccines  to draw another circle of protection. "We made one billion house calls," Brilliant said.

Edward Jenner created his smallpox vaccine in 1796. It took nearly two hundred years, the global cooperation of two superpowers, and the door-to-door efforts of over 150,000 people to end the terror of smallpox. In 1980, the WHO declared that smallpox, the most feared disease in human history, had been eradicated from the face of the Earth. To this day, smallpox is the first and only disease we have completely eradicated.

The Future of Human Health

COVID-19 reminded the world of how interconnected we are, how easy it is for a virus to spread from country to country, to hop oceans, to halt the life of a planet in its tracks. But the pandemic can also serve as a reminder that we are all in this together. Vaccines can save lives, but only if we learn from the past and remember what is at stake.

We now have new tools like CRISPR-Cas9 and mRNA vaccines that scientists are hoping to use to eliminate everything from HIV to mosquito-borne diseases to cancer. We have data analysts using supercomputers to investigate new antiviral treatments that will lessen the length and severity of illnesses. We have initiatives like Canada's Global Public Health Information Network, which is combing the internet to detect news of disease outbreaks before they become epidemics. We have four million people going door-to-door to perform ring vaccinations that will soon eradicate polio.

Humanity still faces a lot of challenges: climate change, rising sea levels, emerging diseases, and barriers to equality. These are not the kinds of challenges that an optimistic country doctor and a sick cow can solve on their own, but because of vaccines we are healthier, we are stronger, and we have a shot at working together to change the world.

How will you use your shot?

GLOSSARY

....

adjuvant: A substance added to a vaccine to trigger and enhance the body's immune response.

antibiotics: A type of medicine, such as penicillin, that kills or stops the growth of microorganisms. Antibiotic chemicals are produced naturally by microorganisms and mold. They are used to treat bacterial infections but have no effect on viruses.

antibodies: Proteins produced by a body's immune system when it detects a foreign substance, such as harmful bacteria, viruses, or fungi. Antibodies find and neutralize the threat to the body.

antigenic drift and shift: The process by which proteins on the surface of a virus mutate gradually (drift) or suddenly (shift) to avoid detection by the host's immune system.

asymptomatic carrier: A person who is infected with a microbe, like a bacteria or a virus, but does not show any symptoms of the disease. Although asymptomatic carriers don't seem to be sick, they can still transmit a disease to others.

atomic: The smallest unit of matter that forms an element.

attenuation: The process of growing generation after generation of germs in a lab to weaken them over time.

bacterium: A living, single-celled microorganism. Unlike viruses, bacteria can reproduce outside of a host body, in places like water, dirt, or on our food. Bacteria exist everywhere on Earth, including on and in the human body. Scientists have identified about 30,000 different species of bacteria, but only about one percent of them actually make people sick.

causative agent: The thing responsible for causing a disease. This can be a bacterium, virus, fungus, parasite, or other microorganism.

chemical: An element or compound that is created through a chemical process.

communicable disease: An illness that spreads from person to person. It can be spread by direct contact with a sick individual, by contact with a sick individual's bodily fluids and respiratory droplets, or by contact with carriers of a disease, such as ticks, lice, or mosquitoes that transport diseases from person to person.

control group: In scientific experiments, subjects are divided into two groups: the control group and the experimental group. The experimental group receives the new type of treatment or vaccine. The control group does not receive any treatment. Scientists compare the results of the two groups to see if the new treatment is working.

culture: A gel or liquid that supports the growth of micro-organisms. Scientists use cultures to reproduce different types of bacteria for experiments. Doctors use cultures to help determine why a person is sick. If you've ever had a test for strep, your doctor might have swabbed your throat and then put your sample in a culture to see if the strep bacteria grew. They determine what type of antibiotic would work best against the infection.

double-blind trial: A experiment where neither the test subject nor the experimenter knows whether the test subject is receiving the thing being tested. This helps to ensure that people's biases and expectations don't corrupt the results of the scientific experiment.

element: In chemistry, this is a pure substance that cannot be broken down into simpler parts by any kind of chemical reaction.

endemic: A disease that is native to the area where people are being infected. The disease was not brought to the area by outsiders.

epidemic: A sudden rise in incidents of a disease in a particular population or region.

fermentation: A chemical process in which bacteria or mold break down sugars and create byproducts such as carbon dioxide and ethanol. In 1856, Louis Pasteur described the fermentation process in wine and identified microorganisms that either helped or ruined wine production.

fungus: Spore-producing organisms, such as mold, yeast, and mushrooms. Fungi are useful as food sources, in food production, and in breaking down natural material. Some types of fungi can cause infections in the human body.

genome: An organism's complete genetic information. The genome is made of DNA, a chemical code that determines any organism's growth and development.

germs: A general term for the tiny organisms that can make you sick. When people talk about germs, they're usually talking about bacteria or viruses.

germ theory of disease: The idea that microscopic organisms, like bacteria and viruses, can spread illness and make people sick. This replaced ideas that sickness came from bad air, an imbalance of bodily fluids called humors, or evil entities like witches or demons.

host: An organism that is infected with a disease or parasite.

immune response: The way a body reacts to a foreign substance, such as harmful bacteria, viruses, or fungi. The immune system recognizes the harmful substance and then attempts to contain and neutralize it. It can also remember germs and infections it has encountered so that it will be prepared to neutralize them in the future.

incubation period: The length of time between when you are infected with a disease and when you will show symptoms of the disease.

infection: An invasion and growth of microorganisms in the body. Common human infections can be caused by bacteria, fungus, viruses, and parasites.

inoculation: The process of introducing a vaccine or other antigen into a body to trigger an immune response that protects the body from a disease.

miasma theory: The idea that breathing in bad or foul-smelling air made people sick. This theory was disproven in the late 1800s by Louis Pasteur and other scientists who demonstrated that germs existed and could cause illness.

microbe: A tiny organism that can only be seen with the use of a microscope or other specialized equipment. Microbes like bacteria and viruses can make people sick.

microorganism: An organism such as a bacterium of microscopic or ultramicroscopic size.

mold: A mass of small fungi that can look hairy or furry. Mold is usually associated with dampness and decay. It is important in breaking down natural materials. Some types of mold have antibacterial properties, such as the mold used to create the widely used antibiotic medication penicillin.

molecule: A group of two or more atoms that are bonded together. For instance, a water molecule is made up of two hydrogen atoms bonded to one oxygen atom (the symbol for this is H_2O). Molecules form the smallest unit of a chemical compound that still retains its properties; an H_2O molecule will still be a liquid at room temperature whether or not there is one or many water molecules. Molecules can be broken into atoms.

organism: An individual, living entity, or thing. Organisms can consist of one cell or be multicellular.

paleovirologist: Someone who studies the remnants of viral material in the DNA of a living organism.

pandemic: A sudden outbreak of a disease that has spread to several countries and continents. If a regional epidemic is not contained or quarantined, it can grow into a pandemic.

parasite: An organism that lives in or on a host's body and benefits at the expense of the host. For example, ticks can attach themselves to a host and feed off their blood. Parasites can also carry diseases that infect the host. Ticks carry the bacterium that causes Lyme disease and can infect their host when they bite.

parent organism: A living entity that can produce an entity similar or identical to itself. Parent organisms replicate genetic material or transfer it to their offspring.

pathogen: A bacterium, virus, or microorganism that can make you sick.

placebo: A harmless substance used in clinical trials for new medicine. The placebo looks like the real treatment, but it is inert. Some common placebos are sugar pills or salt solutions.

post-surgical: Refers to the time after a patient has undergone surgery. Before Joseph Lister introduced antiseptic practices in hospitals in the 1860s, many patients died of post-surgical infections.

proteins: Large, complex molecules that are required for structure, function, and regulation of a body's cells, tissues, and organs. Proteins are present in all living organisms.

ping vaccination or ping immunity: The process of vaccinating people or animals who are near or have been exposed to an infected individual. This vaccination strategy helps cut off vectors for diseases so that it cannot spread to a new host.

serum therapy: A treatment that uses serum, the watery component of blood that is not used in clotting. Medical technicians extract the serum of humans or animals that have developed antibodies to a disease and then deliver it to sick individuals to help their immune system fight that disease.

spore: A reproductive cell that can develop into a new organism. Spores from anthrax are particularly dangerous because they can enter a host and develop into deadly anthrax bacteria.

sterile: Being completely absent of microorganisms such as bacteria, viruses, fungus, or spores.

swan-neck flask: A glass flask with an S-shaped curve at the neck that prevents particles and germs in the air from entering the flask. In the 1860s, Louis Pasteur used a swan-neck flask as part of his experiment to prove the Germ Theory of Disease.

systemic infections: Infections that attack all systems of a body.

toxin: A chemical substance that can damage an organism. Natural toxins can be produced by microorganisms, plants, and animals. In diseases like diphtheria, the bacterium produces a toxin that causes the deadliest symptoms of the sickness. Medical researchers can use the toxin to create Toxoid Vaccines.

toxoid vaccines: Some bacteria produce toxins that can poison their infected host. Medical researchers learned that they could deactivate, or make ineffective, those toxins with chemicals or heat to create a toxoid that cannot cause harm. When used as a vaccine, the toxoid will trigger an immune response from the body without introducing the dangerous bacteria or the toxin that would make an individual sick.

viral drift: Small mutations to a virus's RNA over generations.

viral reassortment: The exchange of RNA that occurs when multiple viruses infect a host cell at the same time. Viral reassortment can lead to changes in how the virus acts, what spike proteins it contains, or what species it infects.

viral shift: Radical, sudden mutations to a virus's RNA.

virulence: The measure of how severe a disease is, or how sick it will make its host.

virus: Nonliving microbes that can enter a host and cause disease. Viruses can only reproduce inside a host. They can infect everything from animals to bacteria.

RECOMMENDED READING

Kehret, Peg. *Small Steps: The Year I Got Polio*. Albert Whitman & Company, 1996.

Marrin, Albert. *Very, Very, Very Dreadful: The Influenza Pandemic of 1918*. Knopf Books for Young Readers, 2018.

Marshall, Linda Elovitz, and Lisa Anchin. *The Polio Pioneer: Dr. Jonas Salk and the Polio Vaccine*. Knopf Books for Young Readers, 2020.

Phelan, Glen. *Science Quest: Killing Germs, Saving Lives: The Quest for the First Vaccines*. National Geographic Children's Books, 2006.

Slade, Suzanne, and Elisa Paganelli. *June Almeida, Virus Detective!: The Woman Who Discovered the First Human Coronavirus*. Sleeping Bear Press, 2021.